WAY OF THE MESSIAH

FOUNDATIONAL TEACHINGS

(Hebrews 6:1-2)

Contents

To begin with, the author of this book is human and makes no claim to inherency.

This being said, it is the author's intent that this book is not simply another book, which expresses the views of the author. Rather, it is his earnest desire that this book points to Scripture, the only source of objective truth.

For this reason, more than 55% of the content in this book is Scripture; and the remaining 40-45% is commentary. Unless otherwise noted, the KJV is used with the Divine names restored, and with the titles "God," "Christ," and "Lord" restored to their original meanings.

To keep this book from getting too lengthy, an explanation of things said is not always provided. It is expected of the readers to look up all Scripture references contained in this book to get such explanation. A Hebrew and Greek concordance (such as Strong's) should also be used. (Blueletterbible.org or software such as e-Sword would also work.)

The readers are also asked not to allow disagreement with content in any chapter(s) to discourage them from reading all chapters of this book.

In the fourth section of this book, the author has expanded the subject of 'Laying on of Hands' to cover several aspects of the local congregation. In the author's views, these aspects are foundational to regaining and maintaining the holiness that the Body of the Messiah once had.

Finally, although chapters 18 and 20 can be helpful, they are not foundational. They can be skipped over.

The Mighty One of Abraham, Isaac and Jacob—the Creator of all things—has many titles, but He only has one name. For verification, see Exo 3:15, 15:3, Isa 42:8, 47:4, 48:2, 51:15, & 54:5, Jer 12:16, 16:21, 31:35, 32:18, 33:2, & 51:19, Amo 4:13, 5:8, & 9:6. Over the years, people have pronounced His name 'Yahweh,' 'Jehovah,' 'Yehovah,' 'Yahuah,' 'Yahveh,' etc. Throughout this book, He will be referred to as 'Yah' for two reasons. One, Scripture calls Him by this shortened form of His name (Exo 15:2, Psa 68:4, Isa 38:11, etc.). Two, and more importantly, not many would argue with this pronunciation. As far as Yah's Son, this book will simply refer to Him as 'Yeshua.' The longer form of this name would be 'Yehoshua' or 'Yahushua,' depending on what vowel points are used (for verification, compare Neh 8:17 with Deu 31:23 and Ezr 3:2 with Zec 6:11), or even 'Yahshua' as a variation. The English name that comes from this Hebrew name is Joshua. The name 'Jesus' is the result of transliterating the Galilean-Aramaic pronunciation of Yeshua: namely 'Yeshu,' with a 's' added to the ending—as was the common practice of dealing with male names ending with a vowel. [Other examples of this practice include Eliyah becoming 'Elias' (Mat 17:3), Jeremiah becoming 'Jeremias' (Mat 16:14), and Zechariah becoming 'Zacharias' (Mat 23:35)]. The 'Y' became an 'I,' which later became a 'J' in English. The 'sh' became a 's,' and the 'u' carried over. Thus 'Yeshu' became Iesu, which then became Iesus, which later became 'Jesus'. Although known that the English names Joshua and Jesus are different names, the later name continues to be used for tradition's sake. The author, however, prefers to use the name His parents and immediate disciples used.

Yah's people are called "saints" nearly 100 times throughout the Bible.

The word *"saint"* ultimately comes from the Hebrew word *"chodesh."*

This word is also behind the words *"holy" "hallow"* and *"sanctify."*

The most literal translation of this Hebrew word is *"set-apart"* or *"separate."*

So if we are Yah's people, we must be "set-apart." We must be "separate."

The command to be "set-apart" is initially given in Exo 22:31 and is repeated five additional times in both the "Old" and "New" "Testaments."

Lev 11:44-45	"be holy for I am holy"
Lev 19:2	"be holy for I am holy"
Num 15:40	"be holy"
Deu 23:14	"be holy"
1 Pe 1:15-16	"be holy in all your conduct because He is holy"

So what does it mean to be holy?

An explanation is provided in ten additional passages of Scripture:

Lev 20:24 & 26	"divided" from all other people
Exo 33:6	"distinguishable" from the people of the earth
Deu 7:6 & 14:2	"chosen to be a treasured people"
Deu 26:19	"high above all nations, in praise, honor and name, for Yah"
Num 23:9	"not counted among the nations"
Eph 1:4 & 5:27	"chosen to be set-apart and without blemish"
1 Pe 2:9	"a chosen people" and "Yah's special possession"

Yeshua says that we have been **called out** of this secular world and that as a result, the secular world would hate us:

Jhn 15:19	"…I have chosen you out of the world"
Jhn 17:14	"…the world has hated them, because they are not of the world"

Regarding our relationship with this secular world, the apostle Paul tells us not to adopt this world's mentality or to be in close relationships with secular people:

Rom 12:2   "Be not conformed to this world"

2Co 6:14, 17   "Be ye not unequally yoked together with unbelievers: for what fellowship has righteousness with unrighteousness? And what communion has light with darkness?

Therefore come out from among them, and be ye separate, says Yah, and touch not the unclean *thing*"

Likewise, the apostle Jacob (aka "James") tells us that we must keep ourselves from the sins of this world and that if we consider this world our friend, we are actually at odds with Yah.

The second part of Jas 1:27, in defining pure religion, he tells us it is to:

"...keep oneself unspotted from the world"

Jas 4:4   "...friendship of the world is enmity with the Mighty One"

Paul also tells us that no believer should be involved in the affairs of this secular world; but instead that we should deny worldly lusts.

2 Ti 2:4 "No man that wars [as a soldier of Yeshua] entangles himself with the affairs of *this* life"

Tit 2:12

"Teaching us that, denying...worldly lusts"

Finally, the apostle John drives the point home:

1 Jo 2:15-17

"Love not the world, **neither the things *that are* in the world**. If any man loves the world, the love of the Father is not in him. For all that *is* in the world, **the lust of the flesh**, and **the lust of the eyes**, and **the pride of life**, is not of the Father, but is of the world. And the world passes away, and the lust thereof"

We can see that the Biblical message of "holiness"—or more accurately translated "set-apartness" is not just a buzzword or a cliché. **It is a calling** that we should not take lightly. Because

"Without...holiness it is impossible to see the Master."

-Heb 12:4

I. Repentance from dead works

Chapter 1

Why He Died

"But the Mighty One commends His love toward us, in that, while we were yet sinners, the Messiah died for us."

- Romans 5:8 (revised KJV)

When presented with the question "why did the Messiah have to die?" many of us would stop for a second to think about the question to try to provide a good, Biblical answer.

"Well, He died for our sins," we might immediately think.

"But what exactly does that mean?" may be the follow-up question in our mind.

"He died to pay the penalty of our sins," may be our final answer.

In church history, this thought is a rather recent development. It traces back to the professor, priest, monk and reformer Martin Luther. The doctrine is called Penal Substitution.

Before this time, Christianity had not taught this. Modern attempts have been made to trace Penal Substitution back to an earlier time. For example, Augustine of Hippo's works are sometimes used in an attempt to link his views to those of the later doctrine. However, such attempts ignore other things that he said that contradict it.

This doctrine, like all church doctrines, must be brought back to Scripture to determine if there is any validity to it.

Does Scripture teach that the Messiah died in our place and thus paid the penalty of our sins, namely death, which we deserved?

A good place to start is a couple of passages that seem to support this notion: 2 Corinthians 5:14, & 1 Peter 2:24.

2 Co 5:14

> "For the love of the Messiah constrained us; because we do judge, that if one **died for all**, then were all dead:"

Taking this verse in isolation, we can see that it seems to say that He died in our place. However, when we read the following couple of verses, we can see that the reason He died for us is so that we can live for Him.

2 Co 5:15-17

> "And *that* he died for all, **that they** which live **should** not henceforth **live** unto themselves, but **unto him** which died for them, and rose again.
>
> Wherefore henceforth know we no man after the flesh: yea, though we have known the Messiah after the flesh, yet now henceforth know we *him* no more.
>
> Therefore if any man *be* in the Messiah, *he is* **a new creature**: old things are passed away; behold, all things are become new."

This same teaching is repeated in the next passage:

1Pe 2:24

> "Who his own self **bare our sins in his own body**
> on the tree, **that we, being dead to sins, should
> live unto righteousness**: by whose stripes ye were
> healed."

This verse brings out more relevant information. Like the
Messiah, who died bearing our sins*, we too, must die to
our sins and live a new life unto Him and His
righteousness.

Rom 6:3-7, 16-18

> "Know ye not, that so many of us as were baptized
> into Yeshua the Messiah were baptized into his
> death? Therefore we **are buried with him by
> baptism into death**: that **like as Messiah was
> raised up from the dead** by the glory of the Father,
> even **so we also should walk in newness of
> life.** For if we have been planted together in the
> likeness of his death, **we shall be also *in the
> likeness* of *his* resurrection**: Knowing this, that
> **our old man is crucified with *him*,** that the **body
> of sin might be destroyed, that henceforth we
> should not serve sin.** For he that is dead is freed
> from sin.
>
> Know ye not, that to **whom ye yield yourselves
> servants to obey, his servants ye are** to whom you

obey; **whether of sin unto death**, <u>or of obedience
unto righteousness</u>? But the Mighty One be thanked,
that **ye <u>were</u> the servants of sin**, but ye have
obeyed from the heart that form of doctrine which
has delivered you. **Being then made free from sin,
ye became the servants of righteousness."**

Here we can see that before we accepted the Messiah as our
Master, we were servants to sin. However, once we are
baptized with Him in His death, we died to our old way of
life and "resurrected" to a new life; a life to be lived for
Him. We became servants of righteousness.

Joh 8:31-36

Then said Yeshua to those Judeans which believed
on him, **"If ye continue in my word,** *then* are ye
my disciples indeed; And ye shall know the truth,
and the truth **shall make you free**." They answered
him, "We be Abraham's seed, and were never in
bondage to any man: how say you, Ye shall be
made free?" Yeshua answered them, "Verily, verily,
I say unto you, **Whosoever commits sin is the
servant of sin**. And the servant abides not in the
house for ever: *but* the Son abides ever. If the Son
therefore shall make you free, **ye shall be free"**

This is the redemption of the Messiah. He purchased us
with His blood (Acts 20:28, Eph 1:7, Col 1:14, Rev 5:9).

We were owned by our own sin (Isa 50:1, Joh 8:34, Rom
6:17). And He freed us (Rom 6:18, 7:5-6, 8:2, Joh 8:36).

Because He redeemed us, we now belong to Him and now
are expected to serve Him. (1 Pe 2:24, Rom 6:18, etc.).

This is the very meaning of the Passover story!

Yah purchased our ancestors with the blood of the Passover lamb.

As a result of the Israelites <u>applying the blood</u> of the lamb to their doorposts, they were redeemed (that is, purchased) from slavery to Egypt.

Exo 6:6

> "Wherefore say unto the children of Israel, I *am* Yah, and <u>I will bring you out from under the burdens </u>of the Egyptians…**I will redeem you**"

Exo 12:13

> "And **the blood shall be to you for a <u>token</u>** upon the houses where ye *are:* and when I see the blood, I will pass over you"

Exo 12:26-27

> "…when your children shall say unto you, What mean ye by this service? That ye shall say, **It *is* the slaughtering of Yah's Passover [lamb],** who passed over…and delivered our houses"

Exo 15:13-16

> "You in your mercy have led forth **the people which you have redeemed**…which **you have <u>purchased</u>**."

Deu 7:8

> "But because Yah loved you…He…brought you out with a mighty hand, and **redeemed you out of the house of bondmen**, from the hand of Pharaoh"

Deu 9:26

> "…which **you have redeemed** through your greatness, which you have brought forth **out of Egypt** with a mighty hand."

Deu 13:5

> "…Yah your Mighty One, which brought you out of the land of Egypt, and **redeemed you out of the house of bondage"**

Deu 15:15

> "And you shall remember that you were a bondman in the land of Egypt, and Yah your Mighty One **redeemed you"**

Deu 24:18

> "But you shall remember that you were a bondman in Egypt, and Yah your Mighty One **redeemed you"**

1 Ch 17:21

> "And what one nation in the earth *is* like your people Israel, whom Yah went to **redeem** *to be* **his own** people…**has redeemed out of Egypt**?"

Psa 74:2

> "Remember your congregation, *which* **you have purchased** of old; the rod of your inheritance, *which* **you have redeemed**"

Psa 106:10

> "And he saved them from the hand of him that hated *them,* and **redeemed them from the hand of the enemy**."

Mic 6:4

> "For I brought you up out of the land of Egypt, and **redeemed you out of the house of servants**"

Lev 25:42, 55

> "For **they *are* my servants**, which I **brought forth out of the land of Egypt**
> …For unto me the children of Israel *are* servants; **they *are* my servants** whom I **brought forth out of the land of Egypt**: I *am* Yah your Mighty One."

The Aramaic Scriptures teach that this redemption story is an analogy for our redemption in Yeshua.

The Passover lamb represents Yeshua (1Co 5:7, 1Pe 1:19).

Egypt represents sin (Act 7:39/Heb 3:14-4:2, 6, 11).

Mar 10:45

> "For even the Son of man came not to be ministered unto, but to minister, and **to give his life a ransom**"

1 Ti 2:6

> "Who **gave himself a ransom** for all"

1 Co 6:20

> "For ye are **bought with a price**: therefore glorify Yah in your body, and in your spirit"

1 Co 7:23

> "Ye are **bought with a price**; be not ye the servants of men."

1 Pe 1:18-19

> "Forasmuch as ye know that ye were not **redeemed** with corruptible things, *as* silver and gold…But **with the precious blood of the Messiah**, as of a [Passover] lamb without blemish and without spot:"

Tit 2:14

> "Who gave himself for us, **that he might redeem us from all iniquity**, and purify unto himself **a** peculiar **people, zealous of good works**."

1 Pe 4:1-2

> "Forasmuch then as **the Messiah has suffered for us** in the flesh...that [we] no **longer should live** the rest of *[our]* time **in the flesh** to the lusts of men, **but to the will of the Mighty One.**"

Eph 2:2, 11

> "Wherein **in time past** ye walked according to the course of this world...children of disobedience
>
> ... ye *being* **in time past** Gentiles

Eph 2:4-6
> **But [now]...in...Yeshua**

Eph 2:13, 10

> **But now in...Yeshua** ye who sometimes were far off are made near **by the blood of the Messiah.**
>
> ... **in... Yeshua** <u>unto good works</u>...that we should **walk in them**"

So why did the Messiah have to die?

There are five reasons.

Four of the five reasons are: **1)** to fulfill prophecy—including Isa 53 and Zec 12:10-14; **2)** to show that He was *The Prophet* by facing the fate of most of the ancient prophets; **3)** to give us the blood of the renewed covenant; **4)** give us an example to follow.

However, the main reason He had to die was to become the ultimate Passover lamb that is the instrument Yah uses to redeem us from our bondage to sin.

We, like the ancient Israelites, must apply His blood to our "doorposts" (that is, our minds) for it to mean anything to us. What this means, is we must <u>always remember</u> that His blood redeems us and saves us from our <u>past sinful life</u> (prior to our conversion).

It is no benefit to us if we continue to sin (2 Pe 1:9, Rom 3:25b, Heb 10:26). This is also taught in Heb 3:14-4:2,6,11 & Jud 1:5.

*bear our sins (1 Pe 2:24; p. 9). This refers to Isa 53:4-6, which in turn, points to the scapegoat of Lev 16:21-22. The Messiah, like the scapegoat, bore our collective sins on Himself. Incidentally, in dying to redeem us, He bore our sins.

He is BOTH the scapegoat of the Day of Atonement AND the lamb of the Passover. While the people did not kill the scapegoat, they did kill the lamb.

Chapter 2
The Prophets

Jer 35:15

> "I have sent also unto you all my servants the
> prophets, rising up early and sending *them,* **saying,**
> **REPENT** ye now every man from his evil way, and
> amend your doings, and go not after other mighty
> ones to serve them, and ye shall dwell in the land
> which I have given to you and to your fathers: **but**
> **ye have not inclined** your ear, nor hearkened unto
> me."

Dan 9:10

> **"Neither have we obeyed** the voice of Yah our
> Mighty One, to walk in **His laws,** which He set
> before us **by his servants the prophets."**

In Mathew 21:33-40, Yeshua tells us a parable in which a
man who planted a vineyard, expected a yield of fruit from
some farmers whom he had entrusted with management of
this vineyard.

When the season was near, he sent his servants to the
farmers to collect fruit. Instead of getting the fruit,
however, he discovered that the farmers had violently
seized and killed the servants whom he had sent.

The man who had planted the vineyard then sent more
servants, with the same intent as he had when he sent the
first ones. When learning that the farmers had done the
same acts of violence to these servants as they had done to

the first, he sent his son with the hope that the farmers would respect his son. Instead, the farmers killed him with the thought that they would receive the sons inheritance.

Yeshua ends his parable with the question:

> *"When the master of the vineyard comes,*
> *what shall he do to those farmers?"*

Five verses later, in Mathew 21:45, we are told that the chief priests and Pharisees understood that this parable was targeted at them. From this then, we can understand that the 'farmers' of this parable were the scribes and Pharisees.

We can also understand that the 'servants' of this parable were the prophets and the 'son' was Yeshua.

This is verified in Mathew 23:29-33 and Luke 11:47-51, where Yeshua accuses the scribes and Pharisees of being the descendants of those who killed the prophets.

And in Mathew 26:14-16, 47/John 18:3/Mathew 27:6, Mathew 27:25 and Acts 5:30 we are told that the high priests and Pharisees were responsible for killing Yeshua.

It doesn't take much, then, to realize that the **man** who planted the vineyard **is Yah**. (Especially in light of what we are told in Psa 80:8-16, Isa 5:1-7 & Jer 12:10)

Nor is it too difficult to figure out that the ***fruit*** of this parable **is obedience** to Yah. (Especially in light of what we are told in Mat 3:10, 7:19, Mar 4:20, Joh 15:8, 16, & Rom 7:4)

Thus, we can understand the parable completely:

Yah entrusted the management of the house of Israel to the leaders of Israel (Gen 49:10, Num 11:14-17, Deu 17:8-13).

He sent prophets to them to get them to obey Him (Jer 7:25, 11:7, 33:15, 44:4, 2Ch 36:15).

They killed His prophets. He sent more. They killed them too (1Ki 19:10, Luk 13:34).

In fact, according to the insight of the author of the book of Hebrews, the prophets experienced mockings, scourgings, bonds and imprisonment, stonings, being sawn in half, being killed with swords, being destitute, afflicted, and tormented, wandering in deserts, mountains, dens and caves in sheepskins and goatskins (11:36-38).

He then sent His only Son, Yeshua, to get the house of Israel to obey Him (Isa 49:6/Mat 15:24, Isa 59:21/Due 18:18/Joh 7:16, 8:28, 8:40, 12:49, 14:24, 17:8, 18:37).

But instead of bearing "fruit worthy of **repentance**," they killed Yah's own Son.

Like most of the former prophets that spoke the Words of the Father to the people and were subsequently killed by the very people to whom they were sent, Yeshua's life and death followed this sequence.

Yeshua is truly the Prophet of Deu 18:15&18!

In fact, repentance is a common theme of the prophets **Isaiah** (1:14, 55:7), **Jeremiah** (3:12,22, 4:1,14, 15:19,

18:8,11, 26:3, 35:15, 36:3) **Ezekiel** (14:6, 18:30), **Hosea** (6:1, 14:1), **Joel** (2:12, 3:7), **Malachi** (3:7), **John the Baptist** (Mat 3:2), **Yeshua** (Mat 4:17, Mar 1:15, 6:12, Luk 13:3, 5, Rev 2:5,22, 3:3,19), **Peter** (Act 2:38, 3:19, 8:22, 2 Pe 3:9), and **Paul** (Act 17:30, 26:20).

All of these Spiritual men preached the same "gospel:"

> *"Repent and turn from your sins;*
> *turn to Yah and He will save you!"*

Chapter 3
Animal Sacrifices

For over 250 years—since the preaching of the American colonist Jonathan Edwards, it has been taught that:

1) Yah instituted animal sacrifices in Gen 3 when He gave Adam and Eve animal skins to cover them after they sinned and ate the fruit.

2) The reason the Mighty One did this was to show that a living creature had to die every time someone sins.

3) This literal death brought about the Mighty One's forgiveness and this pointed to Yeshua, the "ultimate sacrifice."

4) The only reason animals were killed and offered to the Mighty One was for this purpose.

We will address each point in order. But first, it must be brought to attention that the word "sacrifice" is a bad translation that only leads students of the Bible into confusion.

The Hebrew word that has been translated into the word 'sacrifice' is 'zebach' (H2077). The Strong's' Concordance records the primary definition as:

Properly, a slaughter, i.e. the flesh of an animal.

Compare with the Meriam-Webster's primary definition of the word 'sacrifice':

> *The act of giving up something that you want to keep especially in order to get or do something else or to help someone.*

By realizing that the Hebrew word 'zebach' should not be translated as **sacrifice**; but rather **slaughtering**, we are one step closer in finding what the Bible really teaches about this act.

Now we can move on to the four teachings brought up earlier.

1) The Mighty One instituted animal sacrifices in Gen 3 when He gave Adam and Eve animal skins to cover them after they sinned and ate the fruit.

   The underlying reasons this is believed is because:
   a) it is assumed the Mighty One must have killed (an) animal(s) to get animal skins
   b) it is assumed that the Mighty One taught us to offer animals to Him prior to Abel's offering
   c) it is assumed that in the "Old Testament" times, an animal must be killed every time someone sinned against the Mighty One

   The obvious counter to these assumptions is that they are only that—assumptions. The Bible never actually gives these explanations so we end up speculating.

a) The Mighty One does not need to kill an animal to get animal skin. If He created the animal, He can certainly create the animal skin.

b) Abel did, if fact, bring an animal before the Mighty One. Buy why? The Bible doesn't tell us. It only gives us an idea that it may have been a way of tithing or "first fruit offering." The clues given for this idea is Gen 4:3-4 and the use of the words "fruit" (v3) and "firstlings" (v4). What is absent from the account given in Gen 4 is the very thing that would tie it to Gen 3— namely, that sin was the reason they brought the offerings. Rather, Heb 11:4 tells us Abel's offering was simply "gifts."

c) As revealed through His prophets Jeremiah (7:22) and Amos (5:25), during the 40 years the ancient Israelites journeyed in the wilderness, they were not slaughtering animals.*

> *"For I **spoke not** unto your fathers, **nor commanded them** in the day that I brought them out of the land of Egypt, **concerning burnt offerings or slaughtering"***
>
> *"**Have ye offered unto me slaughtering and offerings in the wilderness forty years, O house of Israel?"***

However, Scripture also revealed that during this time when the Israelites were not killing animals, the Mighty One forgave the people no less than ten times. In Numbers 14:19-22, Mosses' prayer to Yah and His answer is recorded:

> *"Pardon, I beseech you, the iniquity of this people according unto the greatness of your mercy, and **as you have forgiven this people**, from Egypt even until now. And Yah said, I have pardoned according to your word...**these ten times"***

So we can see that from the time of Moses, animal bloodshed was not needed for Yah to forgive sins.

This fact is also evident in the writings of the prophets:

2 Ch 7:14

> *"If my people who are called by my name humble themselves, and pray and seek my face and **turn from their wicked ways, then I will** hear from heaven and will **forgive their sin"***

Isa 1:18-19

> *"Come now, and let us reason together,"* says Yah: *"**though your sins be as scarlet, they shall be as white as snow...If ye be willing and obedient"***

Isa 43:25-26

> *"I, even **I, am he that blot out your transgressions** for mine own sake, and will not remember your sins. Put me in remembrance: let us plead together: **confess that you may be justified.**"*

Isa 44:22

> *"**I have blotted out, as a thick cloud, your transgressions, and, as a cloud, your sins: repent**, for I have redeemed you."*

Isa 55:7

> *"Let the wicked **forsake his way**, and the unrighteous man his thoughts: and **let him return** unto Yah, **and He will have mercy** upon him; **and** to our Mighty One, for he will abundantly **pardon.**"*

Jer 36:3

> *"It may be that the house of Judah will hear all the evil which I purpose to do unto them; that they may **return** every man **from his evil way**; that **I may forgive their** iniquity and their **sin.**"*

Jon 3:5,7,10

> *So **the people of Nineveh believed the Mighty One**, and proclaimed a fast, and put on sackcloth, from the greatest of them even*

to the least of them.

*"But let man and beast be covered with sackcloth, and cry mightily unto the Mighty One: yea, let them **turn every one from his evil way**, and from the violence that is in their hands."*

*And **the Mighty One saw their works, that they turned from their** evil way; and **the Mighty One repented of the evil**, that he had said that he would do unto them; and he did it not.*

David, when confessing his sins and asking for forgiveness after the matter of Bathsheba, said that he was not bringing an animal slaughtering to the mighty One; realizing that is not necessary for Yah's forgiveness.

*"For you desire not slaughtering **else would I give** it"*

-Psa 51:16

2) The reason the Mighty One did this was to show that a living creature had to die every time someone sins.

The underlying reason this teaching exists is the belief that the Bible teaches this. The primary passages used to come to this conclusion are Rom 6:23, Eze 18:4&20. *"For the wages of sin is death"* and *"the soul that sins shall die."*

However these verses are speaking of **spiritual** death and not **physical** death.

In Rom 6:23, the contrast is made between sin leading to death, and Yah's gift of eternal life. It is generally not believed that 'eternal life' is literal.

In other words, it is not saying that we will never literally die because we will live forever. Why then, if eternal life is speaking of life after death, is death not likewise speaking of death after death?

In the same way, Eze 18 contrasts 'death' (v4 & v20) and 'life' (v9, v21 & v22). Life is not suggesting that a righteous person will never die; rather, that they will life forever in the life after death. Death therefore, is not speaking of literal death, as both righteous and wicked literally die.

3) This literal death brought about the Mighty One's forgiveness and that this pointed to Yeshua, the "ultimate sacrifice."

This teaching is rooted in a few passages of the "New Testament," which *seem* to say that the death or blood of Yeshua brought about the mighty One's forgiveness.

The primary passages are:

Mat 26:28, Eph 1:7, Col 1:14, 1 Jo 1:7 Heb 9:26 & 10:11-12, 1 Jo 2:2, & 4:10

This is then projected backwards to apply to all animal slaughtering. There are **three** problems with using these passages to reach this understanding.

i) The word used in Mat 26:28, Eph 1:7, & Col 1:14
    that is translated "forgiveness" <u>does not mean
    forgiveness!</u> The word that means forgiveness
    is used in Mat 6:14, Rom 4:17 & 1 Jo 1:9.
    The word used in Mat 26:28, Eph 1:7 & Col 1:14 is
    a <u>different</u> word; a word whose meaning aligns with
    the word redeem. His blood redeems us from our
    bondage to sin; it does not forgive us.

ii) Heb 9:13-14 better explains 1 Jo 1:7 as well as Heb
     9:26 & 10:11-12:

> *"For if the blood of bulls and of goats, and the
> ashes of an heifer sprinkling the unclean,
> sanctifies to the purifying of the flesh. How
> much more shall the blood of the Messiah, who
> through the eternal Spirit offered himself
> without spot to the Mighty One, purge your
> conscience from dead works to serve the living
> Mighty One?"*

What the blood of the animals could do in purifying
the flesh (in the case of the fifth reason identified
below), the blood of the Messiah could do in
purifying the mind. Because of His redemptive
blood, we can now change our conscience—from
our selfish desires to His desires. We go from being
a servant to sin, to a servant of the Mighty One.

This is also taught in 2 Cor 5:15-17, 1 Pe 2:24, 4:1-
2, Tit 2:14, Rom 6:6 & 18, and Gal 3:13.

His blood was the non-monetary (1 Pe 1:18, Isa
52:3) price (Acts 20:28, 1 Cor 6:20, 7:21, Rev 5:9)
for our freedom from our sin (Joh 8:34-36).

iii) The Greek word used in 1Jo 2:2 & 4:10 is often misunderstood as if it means "atoning sacrifice." It is the same word used in the Septuagint for the passages Psa 130:4, Dan 9:9, and Amo 8:14. In the context of these verses, the word means forgiveness. When we repent and accept Yeshua's teaching, we are forgiven.

As demonstrated earlier in point 1c, the death/blood of animals is not needed to bring about the Mighty One's forgiveness. This is further confirmed in Hebrews 10:4 & 11:

> "For *it is* **not possible that the blood of bulls and of goats should take away sins.**"

> "And every priest stands daily ministering and offering oftentimes the same slaughtering, which **can never take away sin:**"

Rather, Scripture teaches:

> Our confession leads to our repentance. (Lev 26:40-41, 1 Ki 8:47/2 Ch 6:37-38, Isa 43:25-26, Dan 9:4, 13)

> Our repentance leads to His forgiveness. (2 Ch 7:14, Job 33:27-28, Psa 32:5, 103:8-12,17-18, 130:3-4, Isa 1:18-19, 44:22, 55:7, Jer 36:3, Eze 18:21, Hos 14:1-4, Jon 3:5,7,10, Mal 3:7, Mar 1:4, Luk 3:3, Act 3:19, 5:31, 11:18, 26:18, 2 Cor 7:10, 1 Jo 1:9)

<u>This, of course, is according to His mercy</u>. (Exo
34:6-7, Num 14:18, Deu 7:9, 2Ch 30:9, Neh 1:5,
9:17, Psa 51:1, 86:5, 103:8-10, Isa 43:25, Lam 3:22,
Dan 9:4, 9, Mic 7:18-19)

If we confess, and repent, **then** He forgives. This
conditional model is consistent throughout Scripture.

4) The only reason animals were killed and offered to the
   Mighty One was for this purpose.

There were five primary reasons animals were killed and
offered to the Mighty One (Lev 7:37):

 i) **To give a gift** (as in the case of the *"meat offering"*
    and in some cases the *"burnt offering"*)
    This is what Cain and Abel brought in Gen 4,
    although no animals were needed to be killed.
    Cain's bloodless gift is called a "meat offering"
    (4:3) just as Abel's was (4:4).This is also what
    Noah did in Gen 8 and Abraham did with Isaac in
    Gen 22. It is also described in Leviticus 1&2. <u>This
    type of offering was not done because of sin.</u>

 ii) **To make a covenant** (as in the case of the
     "sacrifice" and the *"burnt offering"*)
     This is what Jacob did in Gen 31 when making a
     covenant with Laban. <u>This type of offering was not
     done because of sin.</u> This points to Yeshua as He is
     the mediator and messenger of the second, better
     covenant offered to all Yah's people since Moab
     (Deu 29:13ff)

iii) **To give thanks** (as in the case of the *"peace offering"*)
This was first introduced and described in Leviticus 3. This type of offering was not done because of sin.

iv) **To consecrate someone** (as in the case of the *"consecration offering"*)
This was first introduced and described in Exodus 29 and Leviticus 8. This type of offering was not done because of sin. Rather, it was done to set apart the sons of Aaron for the priesthood.

v) **To ask for acceptance and cleansing for inadvertently sinning** (as in the case of the "sin offering" and the "trespass offering" and in some cases the "burnt offering"). This type of offering is described in greatest detail in Leviticus 4. A contrast is made between inadvertent sin (Lev 4:2, 22, &27, Num 15:24,25,26,26,28,&29) and defiant sin (Num 15:30-31). This also points to Yeshua as per Isa 53:10, Heb 9:7, 9:11-12 & 10:26-29. When the animals were killed for this purpose, the sin of the person was not transferred to the animal like our sins were transferred to Yeshua as per Isa 53:4-6, 8 &12. The only time this transfer occurred with an animal, and explicitly stated, was with the scapegoat in Lev 16:21-22, which was not slaughtered but sent away alive into the wilderness.

As can be observed from the list—with exception of number 4, it seems that we (people, not Yah) started killing animals for these reasons and Yah simply allowed it. The first person recorded in Scripture to do it, <u>explicitly stated</u>, was Noah. This was right after the flood. The likely reason he did it was because he had observed it from the secular people just prior to the flood, and thought it was a good idea. The people he learned it from likely learned it from the Nephilim. This was during the time of Enos (Gen 4:26/1Sa 18:24), who was alive during Noah's lifetime (the first 84 years), but not during the lifetimes of Cain and Abel.

Scripture reveals that during the time of the prophets, Yah did not accept animal slaughtering (Isa 1:11, Isa 43:24, Isa 66:3, Jer 6:20, Jer 7:22, Hos 3:4, 8:13, & Amo 5:22).

On certain occasions, the Mighty One did not even accept them from David, who had a genuine heart (Psa 40:6, 50:8-14, 51:16).

However, Scripture also reveals that when the Messiah returns, but before the creation of the new heaven and new earth, Yah will again accept them (Psa 51:19, Isa 56:4-7, Jer 33:18, Mal 3:3-4). This <u>includes</u> the 'sin-offering' (Eze 45:22-25, Eze 46:2, 4, 12, etc.).

When the Mighty One accepts animal slaughtering in the future, they will **not** be done to bring about forgiveness, as they **never** did. That is the purpose of repentance. See also Jer 50:20, and Act 21:18-24, & 26-27.

The fact that Yeshua's sacrifice served an entirely different purpose than the slaughtering of animals is evident in the book of Hebrews.

The author of the book of Hebrews taught that there is a distinction between the covenant given at Sinai founded through the blood of oxen (9:18-21/Exo 24:4-8), typified by the Levitical priesthood (7:11, 8:4, 9:1-9) and the law (7:11, 28, 8:4, 9:19, 10:8), and the renewed covenant (7:22, 8:6, 8, 10, 13, 9:15, 10:9, 16), founded through the blood of Yeshua (9:11-12, 28, 10:10, 19).

Saying this, however, he makes it clear that the Sinai covenant is still in effect (8:13). Thus, the Levitical priesthood (at the time Hebrews was written, prior to the destruction of the Temple) is still in effect (10:3).

Obeying Yah's law or slaughtering animals (the two elements of the Sinai covenant) without Yeshua's blood releasing us from our bondage to sin (2:14-15, 9:12, 14-15) results in an incomplete stature (7:19, 9:9, & 10:1).

However, obeying Yah (and participating in animal slaughtering when Yeshua returns) with the payment of Yeshua's blood, we can be made whole (10:14 & 11:40).

While the book of Hebrews covers several additional topics, in what has been considered the heart of the book (Chapters 7-10) a contrast is made with the two covenants (Deu 29:1, Jer 31:31-32, Rom 9:4, Gal 4:24, Eph 2:12).

There is no contrast made between the "Levitical" or "sacrificial" system and the redemption Yeshua's blood provides.

This conclusion is also consistent with the Biblical concept of atonement.

The Hebrew word that has been translated 'atonement' is used many times in Scripture to refer to the <u>acceptance</u> (or the anticipation thereof) of a gift. This gift could be in the form of <u>live animals</u> (Gen 32:20, Lev 16:10), <u>money</u> (Exo 21:30, 30:15,1Sa 12:3, Amo 5:12), <u>jewelry</u> (Num 31:50) or even <u>prayers</u> (Exo 32:30).

Thus, atonement does not require bloodshed.

Nor does atonement imply forgiveness.

Atonement is made for the alter itself, an inanimate object incapable of sinning (Exo 29:36, 37, Lev 8:15, & 16:18).

*(no slaughtering during the 40 years; p. 23).*This omits the **five** recorded occasions when animals were slaughtered in the wilderness. The reason for the omission is because in four of the five instances when animals were killed, they were done so for other reasons: **1)** 24:4-8 (ratifying the Sinai Covenant), **2)** 40:29/Lev 8/Num 7 (consecrating the Tabernacle), **3)** Lev 8/Num 8 (consecrating the sons of Aaron), and **4)** Num 9 (the second Passover observance). In the final recorded instance of animal slaughtering, it was done as a demonstration (Lev 9-10).

Chapter 4
Circumcision

What does it mean to be circumcised?

If one were to look in a Strong's Concordance of the Bible at the number H4135, they would see:

מוּל <*mool*> A primitive root; to *cut* short, that is, *curtail* (specifically the prepuce, that is, to *circumcise*); by implication to *blunt*; figuratively to *destroy:* - circumcise (-ing, selves), cut down (in pieces), destroy, X must needs.

The range of possible meaning Strong provides here (to cut short, circumcise, blunt, cut down, destroy, etc.) represent how this Hebrew word is translated every time in appears in the Hebrew Scriptures.

The Hebrew word מוּל is used 33 times in the Hebrew Scriptures, but only 24 times this word is used it is referring to the act of cutting off the extra skin that naturally covers the head of the penis.

The first time in Scripture where this word means something other than this literal meaning is in Deu 10:16:

> "Circumcise, therefore, the foreskin of your heart, and be no more stiff-necked."

Here, Yah is commanding the children of Israel to get rid of our stubbornness. When we look at 2Ki 17:14, 2Ch 36:13, Neh 9:16&17, Jer 7:26, Jer 17:23, and Jer 19:15, we can see that stubbornness is the state of the heart/mind of a person when they do not listen to someone that is telling them something. With this understanding in mind, it is easy to see that in Due 10:16, Yah is commanding the children of Israel not to turn our ears away from His words. Now when we place Due 10:16 back in its context of Due 10:12-16, it becomes even more obvious that Yah is telling the children of Israel that the only thing He requires of us is that we love, respect, and obey Him. Therefore, "circumcision of the heart" –as an action performed by us, is obeying Yah (Jer 4:4).

This understanding sheds new light and opens up further understanding on passages of Scripture like: Lev 26:41, Isa 52:1, Jer 6:10, Jer 9:26, & Act 7:51 (which all make use of the word 'uncircumcised' and apply it the those who disobey Yah).

When circumcision was first instituted, it was meant to be the sign of the covenant of Yah on the body of Abraham and his descendants, as well as on the body of those who dwelt with Abraham and his descendants. This practice was continued by Isaac, Israel, and the children of Israel –the Israelites. Therefore, in Jer 9:25, when it is stated that "the days are coming…when I shall punish all circumcised with the uncircumcised" –Yah is using the word מוּל (circumcised) to refer to Israelites while He uses the term ה ערלה (the uncircumcised) to refer to gentiles.

This use of the word also appears in Eze 28:10, 31:18, 32:19&21-32 and is employed many times in the Aramaic Scriptures (Act 10:45, Act 11:2, Act 15:5, Rom 3:1&30, Rom 4:9&12, Rom 15:8, 1Cor 7:19, Gal 2:7-9&12, Gal 5:6, Gal 6:15, Eph 2:11, Phi 3:3, Col 3:11, Col 4:11, Tit 1:10).

Probably the best example of this metaphor being used in the Aramaic Scriptures (aka the "New Testament"), would be Rom 2&3, where Paul explains why he uses it.

In the second chapter of Romans, Paul continues from his message started in Rom 1:17 to the new believers in Rome regarding the false Pharisaic teaching of Mat 16:6&12/Mar 8:15/Luk 12:1 (more specifically Mat 15:3/23:23/Acts 7:53, Mat 23:4/Acts 15:5-10, Mat 23:5-7).

Notice key phrases from Rom 2&3:

"**Therefore**, O man, you are without excuse, everyone who judges, for in which you judge another you condemn yourself, since **you who judge practice the same wrongs**. (hypocrisy!) And we know that the judgment of the Mighty One is according to truth against those who practice such wrongs.

And do you think, O man, you who judge those practicing such wrongs, and doing the same, that you shall escape the judgment of the Mighty One? Or do **you despise the riches of His kindness** (Mat 23:23) and tolerance, and patience, not knowing that the kindness of the Mighty One leads you to repentance?

But according to your **hardness and your unrepentant heart** (Mat 15:1-9/Mar 7:5-13/Act 7:51-53), you are treasuring up for yourself wrath in the day of wrath and revelation of the righteous judgment of the Mighty One, who "shall render to each one according to his works:" everlasting life to those who by persistence in good work seek for esteem, and respect, and incorruptibility; but wrath and displeasure to those who are **self-seeking** (Mat 23:5-7), and **do not obey the truth** (Mat 15:3/23:23) but **obey unrighteousness** (Mat 15:1-9/Mar 7:5-13); affliction and distress on every human being working what is evil, of the Judean first, and also of the Greek; but esteem, respect, and peace to everyone working what is good, to the Judean first and also to the Greek.

For there is no partiality with the Mighty One. For as many as sinned without Law shall also perish without Law, and as many as sinned in the Law shall be judged by the Law.

For **not the hearers of the Law are righteous in the sight of the Mighty One, but the doers of the law shall be declared right** (Mat 5:20/Act 7:53).

 For when gentiles, who do not have the Law, by nature do what is in the Law, although not having the Law, they are a Law to themselves, who show the work of the Law written in their hearts (Deu 10:16/Jer 4:4/Col 2:11); their conscience also bearing witness, and between themselves their thoughts accusing or even excusing, in the day when the Mighty One shall judge the secrets of men through Yeshua the Messiah, according to my good news.

See, **you are called a Jew, and rest on the Law** (Joh 5:39), make your boast in the Mighty One, and know the desire of the Mighty One, and approve what is superior, being instructed out of the Law, and are trusting that you yourself are a **guide to the blind** (Mat 15:14), a light to those who are in darkness, an instructor of foolish ones, a teacher of babes, **having the form of knowledge and of the truth in the Law** (Mar 12:28-34). You, then, who teach another, do you not teach yourself? You who proclaim that a man should not steal, do you steal?

You who say, "Do not commit adultery," do you commit adultery? You who abominate idols, do you rob temples? You who **make your boast in the Law** (Luk 18:11&12), through the **transgression of the Law do you** (Mat 15:3/23:23) disrespect the Mighty One? For the Name of the Mighty One is blasphemed among the gentiles because of you, as it has been written.

<u>For circumcision indeed profits if you practice the Law</u>,

but if you are a transgressor of the Law, **your circumcision has become uncircumcision** (2:5/Mat 15:1-9/Mar 7:5-13/Act 7:51-53). So, if <u>an uncircumcised one watches over the righteousness of the Law</u>), shall not his uncircumcision <u>be reckoned as circumcision </u>(2:15/Deu 10:16/Jer 4:4/Col 2:11)? And the uncircumcised by nature, who perfects the Law, shall judge you who notwithstanding letter and circumcision are a transgressor of the Law!

For he is not a Jew who is so outwardly, neither is circumcision that which is outward in the flesh. But a Jew is he who is so inwardly, and circumcision is that of the heart (2:15/Deu 10:16/Jer 4:4/Col 2:11), in Spirit, not literally, whose praise is not from men but from the Mighty One. What then is the advantage of the Judean, or what is the value of the circumcision? Much in every way! Because firstly indeed, that they were entrusted with the Words of the Mighty One (Psa 147:19&20).

…Or is He the Mighty One of the Judeans only, and not also of the gentiles? Yea, of the gentiles also, since it is one Mighty One who shall declare right **the circumcised** by belief and **the uncircumcised** through belief."

We can see that this passage states that 'the uncircumcised' (gentiles) who watch over the Law, are more 'circumcised' (Jewish) then 'the circumcised' (physical Jews) who disobey the Law. Furthermore, they explain that the term 'circumcised' is simply a term that refers to Jews, whereas the term 'uncircumcised' is a term referring to gentiles.

This helps understand other "New Testament" passages like 1Cor 7:19, where Paul says the same thing he said in his letter to the Romans: that there is no difference between those of the [physical] and those not of the [physical] circumcision, but keeping Yah's commandments is what is important.

If we look at the verse immediately prior to 1Cor 7:19, we are given an important clue in figuring out that Paul was **not** saying that circumcision itself is not important:

"Was anyone called while circumcised? **Let him not become uncircumcised.**
Was anyone called while uncircumcised? Let him not be circumcised." (1 Co 7:18)

A question that may arise in one's mind after reading this verse is "How (and why, if possible) does one become uncircumcised?" The answer to this question should demand the readers' mind to reconsider his/her understanding of the term 'circumcised' and 'uncircumcised,' and point them to the correct understanding of Paul's message here:

"Was anyone called while being Jewish? Let him not become a Gentile.
Was anyone called while being a Gentile? Let him not become Jewish."

So what does it mean to be circumcised?

Two **different** things:

1) To convert to Pharisaic (man-made) Judaism. This is the way it is used in Act 15:5, 1Cor 7:18, Gal 5:1-3 & 6:12-13. This is also described in Gal 2:14, without using the word 'circumcise.'

2) To obey Yah. This is the way it is used in Deu 10:16, 30:6, Jer 4:4, 9:26, Eze 44:7 & 9, Rom 2:15, 26 & 29, & Col 2:11. This would eventually lead to physical circumcision as this is a commandment of Yah (Gen 17:9-14).

Chapter 5

Born Again

What does it mean to be born again?

To answer this question, we will search the Scriptures to find the answer to three sub-questions:

> 1) What is it?

> 2) What does it entail?

> 3) Where is it taught?

1) What is it?

Joh 3:3-8

> Yeshua answered and said to him, "Truly, truly, I say to you, If a man is not **born again**, he cannot see the kingdom of the Mighty One." Nicodemus said to him, "How can an old man be born again? Can he enter again a second time into his mothers womb, and be born?" Yeshua answered and said to him, "Truly, truly, I say to you, If a man is not **born of** water and **the Spirit**, he cannot enter into the kingdom of the Mighty One. What is born of flesh is flesh; and what is **born of the Spirit** is spirit.

> Do not be surprised because I have told you that you all must be **born again**. The wind blows where it pleases, and you hear its sound, but you do not know where it comes and to where it goes; such is every man who is **born of the Spirit**."

Here, Yeshua is equating the phrase "born again" with the phrase "born of the Spirit." The "Spirit," here is to be understood as the Set-apart Spirit or simply Yah (Joh 4:24 & 2 Cor 3:17).

Thus, being "born again" is another way of saying being born of Yah.

2) What does it entail?

1 Jn 2:29

> "If you know that he is righteous, you know also that everyone who does righteousness is [born] of [the Mighty One]."

1 Jn 3:9-10

> "Whoever is **born of the Mighty One** does not commit sin because the Mighty One's seed is in him; and he cannot sin because he is **born of the Mighty One**. In this the children of the Mighty One can be distinguished from the children of the devil: whoever does not practice righteousness and does not love his brother, does not belong to the Mighty One."

1 Jn 5:18

> "We know that everyone who is **born of the Mighty One** does not sin: for he who is born of the Mighty One watches himself, and the evil one does not come near him."

1 Jn 4:7

> "My beloved, let us love one another: for love is from the Mighty One; and everyone who loves is **born of the Mighty One**, and knows the Mighty One."

1 Jn 5:1, 4

> "WHOSOEVER believes that Yeshua is the Messiah is **born of the Mighty One**: and everyone who loves him who begat him, loves him also who is begotten of him.
>
> For whoever is **born of the Mighty One** triumphs over the world: and this is the victory which conquers the world, even our faith."

Here we can see that being 'born again' entails:

- living righteously (in faithful obedience to Yah)

- being unable to sin/being free from sin*

- loving one another

- believing Yeshua is the Messiah

- overcoming the secular mentality of this world by faith

*Being free from sin's bondage and being unable to sin cannot be referring to entering a sinless state, for many Biblical reasons. Rather, it refers to the condition of our heart's desire (Rom 7:15-25). Once we are born of Yah, it is impossible for us *to desire* to disobey Him. Thus, we are unable to sin *willfully*. We have died to our sinful (selfish) intensions. However, this is proved by how we live our entire lives. That is what makes these passages (1Jo 3:9 & 5:18) so difficult to understand. On one hand, the moment we are born again we cannot sin (walk away from Yah). On the other hand, we don't know if we were ever born again until the end of our mortal lives. This could represent looking at it from two different perspectives: Yah's and ours. Only He knows who is truly born again, thus 1 Jo 3:9 & 5:18 make total sense to Him. However for us, they don't make any sense because of what the rest of Scripture teaches (touched on later on in this chapter on pp. 50-54). Perhaps 2Pe 1:10 provides the perfect compromise.

Being born of Yah makes one a child of Yah, thus being born again entails more than this.
(See Joh 1:12-13, Rom 8:16-17, Phi 2:15, & 1Jn 3:1.)

Additionally, being born of Yah also means He dwells in us, which also entails more things.
(See 1 Co 6:16-18 & 2 Co 13:5.)

1 Pe 1:23

> "Being **born again**, not of corruptible seed, but of incorruptible, by the Word of the Mighty One, which lives and abides forever."

Here, Shimon Kepha (Peter) is describing the born-again experience as a transformation from a mortal existence to an immortal existence through the Word of Yah.

Col 3:16

> **"Let the Word** of Messiah **dwell in you** richly,
> **teaching and admonishing one another in all**
> **wisdom"**

1 Th 2:13

> "And because of this we thank the Mighty One
> without ceasing, that when you received **the Word**
> of the Mighty One...which also **works in you"**

When we are born again, not only will we make every
effort to obey and live for Yah as a new creature (2 Cor
5:15-17, Eph 4:22-24, Col 3:9-10), but we allow Scripture,
the Word of Yah and His Messiah, to work in us; teaching
and correcting us in all wisdom.

3) Where (else) is it taught?

Col 2:12

> "And you were buried with him in baptism, and by
> him you were raised with him, for you believed in
> the power of the Mighty One who raised him from
> the dead."

Rom 6:4

> "Therefore, we are buried with him by baptism into
> death: so that as Yeshua the Messiah arose from the
> dead by the glory of his Father, even so we also
> shall **walk in a new life**."

The apostle Paul speaks here of this transformation and
relates it to the baptism of Yeshua (Mat 3:11/Luk 3:16),
that is, the baptism of the Spirit.

Joh 3:9-10

> Nicodemus answered and said to him, "How can
> these things be?" Yeshua answered and said to him,
> "You are a teacher of Israel, and yet you do not
> understand these things?"

Here Yeshua asked Nicodemus how he did not understand
the concept of being born again. It seems as though Yeshua
was expecting this teacher of Torah to grasp this teaching.
Why? Can this teaching be traced to Torah?

Col 2:11-12

> "In Him you were also circumcised with a
> circumcision not made with hands, in the putting off
> of the body of the sins of the flesh, by the
> circumcision of Messiah, having been buried with
> Him in immersion, in which you also were raised
> with Him through the belief"

Here, the Apostle Paul is connecting spiritual circumcision
to the spiritual baptism/rebirth.

In Eze 36:24-28, a prophecy is given that begins with the
future gathering of Israel from among all the nations to
settle us in our own land:

> "And I shall take you from among the Gentiles, and

I shall gather you out of all lands, and I shall bring you into your own land"

This prophecy is also given in Deu 30:3-8 and begins with the same event:

"...He shall...gather you from...the farthest parts under the heavens, from there Yah your Mighty One does gather you...And.. shall bring you to the land which your fathers possessed"

What is interesting is that another event is foretold in each passage:

Eze 36:27

"and **put My Spirit within you**. And I shall cause you to walk in My laws and guard My right-rulings and shall do them."

Deu 30:6

"And Yah your Mighty One **shall circumcise your heart** and the heart of your seed, to love Yah your Mighty One with all your heart and with all your being"

Here, "circumcision of the heart" is equivalent to being given Yah's Spirit.

Although this prophecy is referring to Israel in a corporate sense, whoever circumcises his/her heart allows the Spirit of Yah into his/her life—individually:

Deu 10:16

> "And you shall circumcise the foreskin of your
> heart, and harden your neck no more."

While the concept of removing the "foreskin" of our sinful
self—or more concisely "dying to self," certainly should
point to a particular moment in our lives, it is also *a
process.*

Talking to born again believers, Paul writes:

Col 3:9-10

> "Do not lie one to another, but **put away the old
> life** with all its practices; and **put on the new life"**

Yeshua told His students:

Luk 9:23

> "...If anyone wishes to come after Me, let him deny
> himself, and take up his stake **daily**, and follow Me"

Paul relates, by writing:

1Co 15:31

> "I affirm, by the boasting in you which I have in the
> Messiah Yeshua our Master, I **die day by day**."

2Co 4:16

> "… though our **outward man perish**, yet the
> inward *man* is renewed **day by day**."

Php 1:6

> "being persuaded of this, that He who has <u>begun a good work in you shall perfect it</u> **until** <u>the day of Yeshua the Messiah</u>."

The initial act of repentance and dying to self is the beginning of the born again process. The end of the process is the redemption of our bodies at Yeshua's return:

Rom 8:23

> "And not only so, but even we ourselves who have the first-fruits of the Spirit, **we** ourselves also groan within ourselves, **eagerly waiting for** the adoption, **the redemption** of our body."

Eph 1:14

> "who is the pledge of our inheritance, **until the redemption** of the purchased possession, to the praise of His esteem."

Eph 4:30

> "And do not grieve the Set-apart Spirit of the Mighty One, by whom you were sealed for **the day of redemption**."

The fact that being born again is a process that is not "set in stone" until the end of our mortal lives, is evident in 2 Cor 2:15-16 (NKJV), Phi 2:12, 3:13-14, 1 Cor 9:24-27, Gal 6:7-9, Rom 2:6-7, 1 Pe 1:9; Joh 15:2, 6, Rom 11:20-22, 13:11...

This theme is also discussed throughout the entire book of Hebrews:

2:1

> "give the more **earnest heed** to the things we have heard, **lest we drift away**

2:3

> ...how shall we escape **if we neglect** so great a salvation?

3:6

> ...if we **hold fast...to the end**

3:12

> Beware, brethren, lest here be in any of you...departing from the living Mighty One

3:14

> For we have become partakers of the Messiah **if we hold...to the end.**

4:1

> Let us **fear lest any of you** seem to have <u>come short</u>

4:11

> ...**lest any man fall** after the same example of unbelief

4:14

...**hold fast** our confession

6:4-6

It is impossible for those who were once...partakers of the Set-apart Spirit, **if they fall away**, to renew them again to repentance

6:11

...each one of you show the same **diligence** to the full assurance of hope **until the end**

6:12

...do not become **sluggish**...[but] imitate those who through faith and **patience** inherit the promises

6:18

...**lay hold** of the hope

10:23

Let us **hold fast** the confession of our hope **without wavering**

10:26-27

For **if we sin willfully** after we have received the knowledge of the truth, **there no longer remains**...but a certain **fearful** anticipation of **judgment**

10:31

> ...it is a **fearful** thing to fall into the hands of the living Mighty One.

10:35

> ...**do not cast away** your confidence

10:36

> ...you have need of **endurance, so that...you may** receive the promises

10:38

> ...**if anyone draws back**, My soul has no pleasure in him

Heb 12:3-4

> For consider him that **endured** such contradiction of sinners against himself, **lest ye be wearied** and faint in your minds. Ye have not yet resisted unto blood, **striving against sin**.
>
> Looking **diligently lest any man fail** of the grace of the Mighty One; lest any root of bitterness springing up trouble *you,* and thereby many **be defiled;**"

II. Faith Toward Yah

Chapter 6

Definition of Faith

Faith, as the Bible describes it, has two parts.

Part 1

In one word, the Strong's Concordance to the "New Testament" defines the Greek word (G4102) for faith as *belief.* In fact, most major translators (KJV, YLT, NLT, NIV, etc.) translate this Greek word as belief in 2 Thes 2:13:

> "… because the Mighty One has from the beginning chosen you to salvation through sanctification of the Spirit and **belief** [G4102] of the truth"

In addition to the way it is used in the above passage, it is used this way in the following passages:

Gal 3:6-7

> "according as Abraham did **believe** the Mighty One, and it was reckoned to him -- to righteousness; know ye, then, that those of **faith** -- these are sons of Abraham"

Heb 11:6

> "and apart from **faith** it is impossible to please well,
> for it behooves him who is coming to
> the Mighty One to **believe** that He is, and to those
> seeking Him He becomes a rewarder."

Jam 2:18-20

> "But someone may say, You have **faith**, and I have
> works, show me your faith out of your works, and I
> will show you out of my works my faith: you -- you
> **believe** that the Mighty One is one; you do well,
> and the demons believe, and they shudder! And do
> you wish to know, O vain man, that the **faith** apart
> from the works is dead?"

So faith is belief. If one believes in Yah, they have faith in Yah. If one believed the "Gospel," one has faith in the "gospel."

The "Gospel" is often condensed into a single verse, John 3:16:

> "For the Mighty One so loved the world that he
> gave his only begotten son, that whosoever believe
> in Him should not perish but have eternal life."

Yah gave mankind the gift of salvation. All we have to do is accept that gift by believing in His Son.

Put another way, Yah's grace is given freely to all who have faith in His Son. This, of course is a re-wording of Eph 2:8-9:

> "For you have been saved by grace through faith. It is a gift of the Mighty One; not of works lest any man should boast."

Part 2

Although in its most basic sense, the word faith simply means belief, faith has a deeper meaning. If we truly believe that Yeshua is the Master, we would accept Him as our Master. If we make Him our Master, then we will naturally want to obey Him. After all, if He is our Master, that makes us His servants. What kind of servant does not obey the one which he accepts as his master? This is exactly what the Messiah said in Luke 6:46:

> "Why do you call me Master, and do not do what I say?"

So by putting our faith in the Messiah, we should naturally desire to obey Him. Put another way, our faith in Him produces acts of obedience. Faith produces works. This is precisely what both Jacob (aka James) and Paul say:

Eph 2:8-10

> "...**through faith**...For we are his workmanship, created in the Messiah Yeshua **unto good works**, which Yah has before ordained that we should walk in them."

Jam 2:18

> "Yea, a man may say, You has faith, and I have
> works: shew me your faith without your
> works, and I will shew you my **faith by my
> works**."

So we can see that genuine faith has two parts. It starts with belief; and this belief produces works.

So why does it seem like Paul contrasts faith and works; if in fact, they work together?

Rom 3:27

> "Where *is* boasting then? It is excluded. By what
> law? **of works**? Nay: **but** by the law **of
> faith**."

Gal 2:16

> "Knowing that…we might be **justified by the
> faith** of the Messiah, and **not by the works** of
> the law: for by the works of the law shall no flesh
> be justified."

It is because the majority of the bloodline descendants of Jacob/Israel had lost the faith, but kept the works. As Paul explained:

Rom 9:31-32

> "But Israel, which followed after the law of
> righteousness, has **not attained to the law of
> righteousness.** Why? **Because** *they sought it* not

<u>by faith</u>, **but** as it were <u>by the works</u> of the law."

This explains why Yeshua said:

Mat 23:23

> "Woe unto you, scribes and Pharisees, hypocrites!
> for ye pay tithe of mint and anise and
> cummin, and **have omitted** the weightier *matters*
> of the law, judgment, mercy, and **faith**:
> these ought ye to have done, and not to leave the
> other undone."

They lost sight of the whole point of the law: Yah's righteous judgments, His loving mercy, and the faith He requires of us.

In other words, they missed out on the love Yah shows us in giving us righteous judgments.

Luk 11:42

> "But woe unto you, Pharisees! For **ye** tithe mint and
> rue and all manner of herbs, and **pass over**
> judgment and the **love of Yah**: these ought ye
> to have done, and not to leave the other undone."

Unfortunately, ***this*** point is missed by the majority of Christians. Yah's law is not a bad thing. The opposite is true!

As Paul explains in Rom 7:12, 16 & 1 Tim 1:8:

> "Wherefore the law *is* holy, and the commandment holy, and just, and good."

> "… the law that *it is* good."

> "But we know that the law *is* good, if a man use it lawfully"

The reason Paul seems like he says otherwise in his letters is that his audiences were first century believers who were influenced by Pharisaic Judaism's teaching that all one had to do was good things and follow <u>them</u>. Paul put an emphasis on faith because the Pharisees and <u>their</u> followers did not have faith in Yah.

If we are **obeying** Yah's law **<u>by faith</u>**, we are righteous (another word for *<u>just</u>*) in His eyes:

Rom 2:13

> …the **doers of the law** shall be <u>justified</u>

Rom 3:30-31

> "Seeing *it is* one Mighty One, which shall <u>justify</u> the circumcision [Jews by bloodline] **by faith**, and uncircumcision [Gentiles by bloodline] **by faith**.

> <u>Do we then make void the law through faith?</u> The Mighty One forbid: nay, **we establish the law**."

In fact, the righteous have always lived by faith!

(Hab 2:4, Heb 11:4-39)

III. Teaching of Baptisms

Chapter 7
The Baptism of John

Luk 3:1-2

> Now in the fifteenth year of the reign of Tiberius
> Caesar...<u>the word of the Mighty One came unto</u>
> <u>John</u> the son of Zacharias in the wilderness.

Mat 3:1-6

> In those days came John the Baptist, preaching in
> the wilderness of Judaea, and saying, "<u>Repent ye:</u>
> <u>for the kingdom of heaven is at hand</u>." For this is he
> that was spoken of by the prophet Esaias, saying,
> "The voice of one crying in the wilderness, Prepare
> ye the way of Yah, make his paths straight." Then
> <u>went out to him Jerusalem, and all Judaea, and all</u>
> <u>the region round about Jordan,</u> and <u>were baptized of</u>
> <u>him in Jordan, confessing their sins.</u>

Joh 1:19,26, 33

> And this is the record of John, when the Judeans
> sent priests and Levites from Jerusalem to ask him,
> "<u>Who art you?</u>"

> John answered them, saying, "I baptize with water:

> And I knew him not: but he that sent <u>me to baptize</u>
> <u>with water</u> [unto repentance- Mat 3:11]"

Baptism in water is associated with preaching confession and repentance. This is demonstrated in the following passages:

Joh 4:1-2

> When therefore the Master knew how the Pharisees had heard that Yeshua <u>made and baptized more disciples than John,</u> (Though Yeshua himself baptized not, but his disciples,)

Mar 1:14-15

> Now after that John was put in prison, Yeshua came into Galilee, preaching the gospel of the kingdom of the Mighty One, and saying, "The time is fulfilled, and the kingdom of the Mighty One is at hand: **repent** ye, and believe the gospel."

Mat 4:17

> From that time Yeshua began to preach and to say, "<u>Repent: for the kingdom of heaven is at hand</u>."

When John was imprisoned, Yeshua and His disciples were preaching repentance, baptizing new disciples with water.

Luk 7:29-30

> And all the people that heard *him*[Yeshua], and the publicans, justified the Mighty One, <u>being baptized with the baptism of John</u>. But the Pharisees and lawyers <u>rejected the counsel of the Mighty One</u> against themselves, being <u>not baptized of him</u>.

The Pharisees and lawyers refused to confess their sins and be baptized with water by John. Thus, they rejected what Yeshua had to say.

The fact that baptism in water was preaching repentance also explains why the earliest disciples paraphrased Yeshua's instructions given in Mathew 28:19-20

> "Go ye therefore, and teach all nations, baptizing them in the name...teaching them to observe all things whatsoever I have commanded you"

In Luk 24:47 as

> "And that repentance and remission of sins should be preached in his name among all nations, beginning at Jerusalem."

The words "teach/preach," "in the/his name," and "all nations" are present in both passages. Thus, "baptizing" (Mat 28:19) is understood as preaching "repentance" (Luk 24:47).

This later paraphrase of the so-called "great commission" is carried out in Acts 26:20:

> "But shewed first unto them...at Jerusalem, and throughout all the coasts of Judaea, and then to the Gentiles, that they should repent and turn to the Mighty One, and do works worthy of repentance."

In the first six verses of the 19th chapter of the book of Acts, a clear distinction is made between John's baptism with water and Yeshua's baptism with His Set-apart Spirit:

> And it came to pass, that, while Apollos was at Corinth, Paul having passed through the upper coasts came to Ephesus: and finding certain disciples, He said unto them, "Have ye received the Set-apart Spirit since ye believed?" And they said unto him, "We have not so much as heard whether there be any Set-apart Spirit." And he said unto them, "Unto what then were ye baptized?"
>
> And they said, "Unto John's baptism." Then said Paul, "John verily baptized with the baptism of repentance, saying unto the people, that they should believe on him which should come after him, that is, on the Messiah Yeshua." When they heard *this,* they were baptized in the name of the Master Yeshua. And when Paul had laid *his* hands upon them, the Set-apart Spirit came on them

Here we can see that these early disciples were baptized with John's baptism of repentance, but were in need of Yeshua's baptism to receive the Set-apart Spirit of Yah. We can also see that this took place after Pentecost, the original receiving of the Set-apart Spirit of Yah (Act 1:5, 2:33).

This distinction is also present in Act 8:12-16:

> But when they believed Philip preaching the things concerning the kingdom of the Mighty One, and the name of Yeshua the Messiah, they were baptized, both men and women. Then Simon himself believed also: and when he was baptized, he continued with

Philip, and wondered, beholding the miracles and signs which were done.

Now when the apostles which were at Jerusalem heard that Samaria had received the word of the Mighty One, they sent unto them Peter and John: who, when they came down, prayed for them, that they might receive the Set-apart Spirit: (For as yet he [the Set-apart Spirit] was fallen upon **none** of them: [for] they were only baptized in the name of the Master Yeshua.)

This distinction is further verified in Acts 10:47-48:

"Can any man forbid water, that these should not be baptized, which have received the Set-apart Spirit as well as we?" And he commanded them to be baptized in the name of the Master. Then prayed they him to tarry certain days.

It this case, these early disciples had been baptized with Yeshua's baptism of the Set-apart Spirit, but not John's baptism of water. This bizarre order is also present in Act 2:38 & 41, which took place after the baptism of the Spirit (1:5 & 2:33).

This is precisely what John meant when he said:

"I indeed have baptized you with water: but he shall baptize you with the Set-apart Spirit."

-Mat 3:11, Mar 1:8, Luk 3:16, Joh 1:26, 33.

John's baptism was with water (Joh 1:19, 26, 31, 33, 3:23,

Luk 3:16, Act 1:5, 11:26). It was preaching repentance
(Mat 3:2, 11, Act 10:37) and was accompanied by
confession (Mat 3:6). This is why it is called "the baptism
of repentance" (Mar 1:4, Luk 3:3, Act 13:24).

What we must understand is that while all are commanded
to "let our light shine" through our actions (Mat 5:16), not
all are given the commission to baptize and make disciples
(Mat 28:19-20). Paul—an early disciple and apostle, for
example, was **not** given the commission to baptize with
water and make disciples. As recorded in 1Co 1:17:

> "For the Messiah sent me not to baptize, but to
> preach the gospel"

What should also be understood by those who *are* called to
preach repentance and baptize new disciples is that the
original reading of Mat 28:19, in all <u>known</u> Hebrew, Greek
and Aramaic/Syrian manuscripts, has been altered. The
original reading is only preserved throughout the book of
Acts.

Act 2:38

> Then Peter said unto them, "Repent, <u>and be</u>
> <u>baptized</u> every one of you <u>in the name of Yeshua</u>"

Act 8:16

> (For…they were <u>baptized in the name of the Master</u>
> <u>Yeshua</u>.)

Act 10:48

> And he commanded them to be <u>baptized in the name of the Master</u>.

Act 19:5

> When they heard *this,* they were <u>baptized in the name of the Master Yeshua</u>.

Act 22:16

> "And now why wait? Arise, and <u>be baptized</u>, and wash away your sins, calling on <u>the name of the Master</u>."

There was no 'Trinitarian formula' being used in water baptisms in the book of Acts!

Chapter 8
The Baptism of Yeshua

Unlike the baptism of John—which is what most of us that have a background in Christianity have heard of, the baptism of Yeshua is an entirely different thing. According to the following passages, His baptism was His death!

Luk 12:50

> "But I have a **baptism** to be baptized with; and how am I straitened till it is accomplished!"

Mat20:22-23

> But Yeshua answered and said, "Ye know not what ye ask. Are ye able to drink of the cup that I shall drink of, and to be baptized with the **baptism** that I am baptized with?" They said "we are able."
>
> And he said unto them, "Ye shall drink indeed of my cup, and be baptized with the **baptism** that I am baptized with"

Rom 6:3-4

> "Know ye not, that so many of us as were baptized into Yeshua the Messiah were baptized **into his death**? Therefore we are buried with him by baptism into death: that like as the Messiah was raised up from the dead by the glory of the Father, even so we also should walk in newness of life."

Col 2:12

> "Buried with him in **baptism**, wherein also ye rise
> with *him* through the faith of the operation of the
> Mighty One, who has raised him **from the dead**."

When we are baptized with Him, we are baptized onto
death. While His death was literal, ours is figurative.

We die to our own selfish desires; that is, our sinful nature.
This is another way of saying we deny ourselves and be
prepared to be figuratively crucified. This is what He was
saying in Mat 16:24 & Mar 8:34:

> "If any *man* will come after me, let him **deny
> himself**, and take up his *stauros*, and follow me."

This is also what He meant in John 12:24, when He said:

> "Except a corn of wheat fall into the ground **and
> die**, it abides alone: but if it die, it bring forth much
> fruit."

In addition to dying to self, Yeshua's baptism is also
referred to as being baptized with the Set-apart Spirit. In
what has been called the "New Testament," this was first
realized at Pentecost.

Act 1:5

> "…but ye shall be baptized with the Set-apart Spirit
> **not many days from now**."

Act 2:33

> "...having received of the Father <u>the promise of the Set-apart Spirit</u>, he has shed forth this, **which ye now see and hear**."

This baptism is appropriately called "baptism of the Set-apart Spirit;" for when the new disciple is baptized with this baptism, they are given the Set-apart Spirit. In most of the examples given in the book of Acts, this happened either <u>after</u> John's baptism or skipping it altogether.

Act 8:13-17

> Then Simon himself believed also: and <u>when he was baptized</u>, he continued with Philip, and wondered, beholding the miracles and signs which were done. Now when the apostles which were at Jerusalem heard that Samaria had received the word of the Mighty One, they sent unto them Peter and John: who, when they were come down, prayed for them, that **they might receive the Set-apart Spirit**: (For as yet he was fallen upon none of them: [for] <u>they were only baptized in the name of the Master Yeshua</u>.) Then laid they *their* hands on them, **and they received the Set-apart Spirit**.

Act 11:15-16

> "And as I began to speak, the **Set-apart Spirit fell on them**, <u>as on us at the beginning</u>. Then remembered I the word of the Master, how that he said, 'John indeed baptized with water; but **ye shall be baptized with the Set-apart Spirit**.'"

Act 16:15

> And when <u>she</u> [a certain woman named Lydia] **was baptized**, <u>and her household</u>, she besought *us,* saying, If ye have judged me to be faithful to the Master, come into my house, and abide *there.* And she constrained us.

Act 16:33

> And <u>he</u> [The Philippian Jailer] took them [Paul and Silas] the same hour of the night, and washed *their* stripes; and **was baptized**, he and all his, immediately.

Acts 19:5-6

> …When they heard this, **they were baptized in the name of the Master Yeshua.** And when Paul had laid his hands upon them, **the Set-apart Spirit came on them**

The baptism of the Set-apart Spirit is linked to dying to self because when we die to self, we are given His Spirit.

Rom 8:13

> "…but if ye **through <u>the Spirit</u> do mortify the deeds of the body**, ye shall live."

2 Co 5:15-16

> "And that he died for all, that they which live should **not henceforth <u>live unto themselves</u>, but unto him** which died for them...know we [were] no man after the flesh. **Yet now** henceforth **know we** him **[our old man] no more**."

Eph 4:22-24

> "That ye **put off...the old man**, which is corrupt according to the deceitful lusts...And that ye **put on the new man"**

Col 3:8-10

> "But now ye also **put off** all these...**the old man** with his deeds; And have **put on the new man"**

Rom 6:4

> "... as the Messiah was raised up **from the dead** by the glory of the Father, even so, **we also should <u>walk in</u> newness of life**."

Gal 5:24-5

> "And they that are the Messiah's **have crucified the flesh** with the affections and lusts. If we live in the Spirit, **let us** also <u>walk in **the Spirit**</u>."

Everyone who is baptized with this baptism of death to self is baptized in His Spirit. This new, reborn person becomes part of the Body of the Messiah.

Gal 3:27

> "For as many of you as have been **baptized** into the Messiah have **put on** the Messiah."

1Co 12:13

> "For **by one Spirit are we all baptized into one Body**"

Eph 4:5

> "One Master, one faith, **one baptism**"

This is the baptism that is essential for salvation.

Joh 3:3

> Yeshua answered and said unto him, "Verily, verily, I say unto you, **except a man be born** again [**of the Spirit**—v8], **he cannot see the kingdom** of the Mighty One."

Mar16:16

> **"He that** believeth and **is baptized shall be saved**; but he that believeth not shall be damned."

1Pe 3:21

> "The like figure whereunto *even* **baptism doth also now save us** (not the putting away of the filth of the flesh, but the answer of a good conscience toward the Mighty One,) by the resurrection of Yeshua the Messiah:"

While John's baptism is about *preaching* repentance and making new disciples, Yeshua's baptism is about *an individual* repenting—turning to Yah and putting to death our former way of life.

IV. Laying on of Hands

Chapter 9

Leadership in the Assembly

The Biblical government structure of His Assembly is as follows:

The Head = Yeshua

Eph 4:15

> "but, maintaining the truth in love, we grow up in all respects into Him who is **the head, Messiah**,"

Eph 5:23

> "Because the husband is head of the wife, as also the **Messiah is head...**of **the body**."

Notice how it says that Yeshua is the head of this Body. This is consistent with what He taught in Mat 23:8-11.

The Body = the Assembly

Col 1:18

> "And **He is the Head of the body, the assembly**"

Col 1:24

> "...for the sake of **His Body**, which is **the assembly**"

Eph 5:23

.   "the Messiah is head of **the assembly...of the body**."

His role:

Eph 5:29

"For no one ever hated his own flesh, but **feeds and cherishes** it, as also the **Master does the assembly**."

Yeshua feeds and cherishes His assembly. This is referring to spiritual food and nourishment (i.e. teaching of the Word).

Assembly Member's roles:

Collective:

Eph 5:21

"subjecting yourselves to each other in the fear of the Mighty One."

1Co 12:25

"the members should have the same concern one for another."

Each congregational member must subject themselves to each other and have the same degree of concern for one another. This falls in line with what Yeshua taught in Mat 20:26-27 & 23:11.

Individual:

1Co 12:12-18

> "For as the body is one and has many members, but **all the members** of that **one body**, being many, are one body, so also is **the Messiah.**
>
> For indeed by one Spirit we were all immersed into one body, whether Yahudim or Greeks, whether slaves or free, and we were all made to drink into one Spirit.
>
> For indeed **the body** is **not one member but many.**
>
> If **the foot** says, "Because I am not **a hand**, I do not belong to the body," does it therefore not belong to the body? And if **the ear** says, "Because I am not **an eye**, I do not belong to the body," does it therefore not belong to the body? If all the body was an eye, where would be the hearing? If all hearing, where would be **the smelling**?
>
> But now the Mighty One has set the members, each one of them, in **the body**, even as He pleased."

Each member of the Assembly has a different individual gift, just as a body has different body parts each serving their respective function. Each member of the Assembly has an equally important role in the overall function of the Body.

1Co 12:23-24

> "And to **those of the body which we think to be less respected, these we present greater respect**. And our unseemly *members* have greater seemliness, whereas our seemly *members* have no need.
>
> But **the Mighty One blended together the body**, having **given greater** respect to that *member* which lacks it,"

More respect should be given to the ones thought to be of the seemingly lowest significance to the Body because these are the ones Yah gives greater respect. This is exactly what Yeshua taught in Mat 19:30 & 20:16.

1Co 12:27-30

> "And **you are a body of Messiah**, and members individually. And the Mighty One has appointed these in **the assembly**:
>
> firstly **emissaries**, secondly **prophets**, thirdly **teachers**, after that miracles, then gifts of healings, helps, ministrations, kinds of tongues.
>
> Are all emissaries? Are all prophets? Are all teachers? Are all **workers of miracles**? Do all have **gifts of healings**? Do all **speak with tongues**? Do all **interpret**?"

Here, the apostle Paul said that there were certain individuals in the first century Assembly that were appointed:

1) apostles
2) prophets
3) teachers

Then,

> -workers of miracles
> -healers
> -givers of relief
> -directors
> -speakers of tongues
> -interpreters of tongues

Reading through the book of Acts, one can observe that in many cases more than one of these gifts were given to a single individual. For instance, Steven was a worker of miracles (6:8) as well as an evangelist (7:2-54). Philip was an evangelist (8:5), a miracle worker (8:6) as well as a teacher (8:30-35). All the apostles and others were speakers of tongues (2:4) and many became prophets, evangelists, teachers, givers of relief, workers of miracles, directors, and so forth. Paul was an apostle as well as an evangelist, teacher, healer, and a miracle worker. All members were capable of having one, or all, of these gifts. Today, however, these gifts should not be used or treated as an office or title.

Leadership:

Act 13:2, 14:23

> And as they were doing service to the Master and fasted, the Set-apart Spirit said, "Separate unto Me Barnaḇah and Sha'ul for the work to which I have

called them." ...And [they] **appointed elders in
every assembly**, having prayed with fasting, they
committed them to the Master in whom they had
believed.

Act 20:17-18, 28

And from Miletos he sent to Ephesos and called for
the **elders of the assembly.** And when they had
come to him, he said to them,

"...Therefore take heed to yourselves and to all the
flock, among which the Set-apart Spirit has made
you overseers, to **shepherd the assembly of the
Mighty One** which He has purchased with His own
blood."

1Pe 5:1-2

"...I appeal **to the elders among you:**

Shepherd the flock of the Mighty One which is
among you, **serving as overseers,**"

The elders of each location of His Assembly are the ones
who are responsible for shepherding and overseeing His
Assembly.

Tit 1:5-10

"The reason I left you in Crete was that you should
straighten out what was left undone, and **appoint
elders in every city** as I appointed you:

if any be

1) proven worthy,
2) the **husband** of one wife,
3) **having believing children** not accused of loose behavior, or unruly.
4) not self-pleasing,
5) not wroth,
6) not given to wine,
7) no brawler,
8) not greedy for filthy gain,
9) but kind to strangers,
10) a lover of what is good,
11) sensible,
12) righteous,
13) set-apart,
14) self-controlled,
15) clinging to the trustworthy word, according to the teaching, to be able both to **encourage by sound teaching, and to reprove those who oppose it**."

1Pe 5:2-3

16) "not by compulsion but voluntarily, not out of greed for filthy gain, but eagerly,
17) neither as being masters over those entrusted to you, but being examples to the flock."

As it can be seen above, there are many qualifications one must meet to receive this position of leadership. One such requirement is to be capable of giving sound Biblical teaching and reproof to the Assembly.

What can also be learned is that each Assembly is to have elder<u>s</u> (plural) to oversee and shepherd the congregation. They are the instruments Yeshua uses to sustain her.

This is necessary for the protocol of Mat 18:15-20/1Co 5:11-13, Ja 5:14-15, Heb 13:17, & 1 Ti 5:17-19 to be followed. This is also necessary to enforce the protocols of 1 Ti 5:1-10 & 1 Pe 5:5.

The one other position is the 'servant' calling of 1Ti 3:8-13. As it can be observed below, this position has about half of the qualifications as that of the elder position.

1Ti 3:8-12

> "Likewise servants (translated 'deacons') are to be
>
> 1) reverent,
> 2) not double-tongued,
> 3) not given to much wine,
> 4) not greedy for filthy gain,
> 5) holding to the secret of the belief with a clean conscience.
> 6) And let these also be proved first, then let them serve, if they are proven worthy.
> 7) Let [the] servants be the **husbands** of one wife,
> 8) ruling children and their own houses well."

However, unlike the elders, the position of servant is not one of authority. They do not oversee or shepherd the congregation as the elders do. Conversely, as the name implies, they serve the congregation. To get a better idea of what this word means, it is the same word used in Luk 22:26 and Act 6:2.

Beyond the office of elder—that is held by at least <u>two different married (or widowed) men</u>, and the office of servant—which is not a leadership role, there is no other Biblically based office within the Assembly.

There is no office of 'Pastor,' 'Reverend,' 'Rabbi,' or any other name given to an office held by a single individual.

Chapter 10
Tongues and Tithes

This chapter is naturally divided into two sections: tongues, and tithes.

Tongues

The first incident of people speaking in tongues in the "New Testament" is in Acts 2:1-8:

> And when the day of Pentecost was fully come, they were all with one accord in one place. And suddenly there came a sound from heaven as of a rushing mighty wind, and it filled all the house where they were sitting. And there appeared unto them cloven **tongues like as of fire**, and it sat upon each of them.
>
> And **they** were all filled with the Set-apart Spirit, and **began to speak with other tongues**, as the Spirit gave them utterance. And there were dwelling at Jerusalem Jews, devout men, **out of every nation under heaven**. Now when this was noised abroad, the multitude came together, and were confounded, because that **every man heard them speak in his own language**.
>
> And they were all amazed and marveled, saying one to another, Behold, are not all these which speak Galilaeans? And how **hear we every man in our own tongue**, wherein we were born?

It can clearly be seen here that this speaking in "tongues" was nothing more than speaking in different languages.

Additionally, everybody present understood what was being said because they were speaking in <u>known</u> languages.

There are two different Greek words that are translated "tongues" in the "New Testament" that are represented by the Strong's numbers G1100 and G1258. Both these words are used to mean *language* in Acts 2. This supernatural ability to speak in different known languages was given with the baptism of the Set-apart Spirit (2:4).

The next two times this ability is given is also accompanied with the baptism of the Set-apart Spirit.

Act 10:45-46

> ...on the Gentiles also was poured out the gift of **the Set-apart Spirit**. For they heard them **speak with tongues**, and magnify the Mighty One

Act 19:6

> And when Paul had laid his hands upon them, the **Set-apart Spirit** came on them; and they **spoke with tongues**, and prophesied.

The next place this ability is spoken of is 1 Corinthians 12, where it is listed with the other Spiritual gifts (v10, v28 & v30). Unlike the examples in the book of Acts, however, in the context of 1 Corinthians the ability to speak in a different language is such that the language cannot be understood unless an interpreter is present.

The principle passage that deals with the "Spiritual gift" of speaking in an unknown language is 1 Corinthians 14.

1Co 14:1-22, 27-28, 33

"Follow after charity, and desire **spiritual** *gifts,* but rather that ye may prophesy. For he that **speaks in** an *unknown* **tongue** speaks not unto men, but unto the Mighty One: for **no man understands** *him;* howbeit in the spirit he speaks mysteries.

But he that prophesy speaks unto men *to* edification, and exhortation, and comfort. **He that speaks in an *unknown* tongue edifies himself**; but he that prophesy edifies the Assembly.

I wish *not* that ye all speak with tongues, but rather that ye prophesied: for greater *is* he that prophesy than he that speaks with tongues, **except he interpret**, that the Assembly may receive edifying.

Now, brethren, if I come unto you speaking with tongues, what shall I profit you, except I shall speak to you either by revelation, or by knowledge, or by prophesying, or by doctrine?..So likewise ye, **except ye utter by the tongue words easy to be understood,** how shall it be known what is spoken? for **ye shall speak into the air**…shall be unto him that speaks a barbarian, and he that speaks *shall be* a barbarian unto me. Even so ye, forasmuch as ye are zealous of spiritual *gifts,* seek that ye may excel to the edifying of the Assembly.

Wherefore let him that speaks in an *unknown* tongue **pray that he may interpret**. For if I pray in an *unknown* tongue, my spirit prays, but my **understanding is unfruitful.**

…I thank my Mighty One, I speak with tongues more than ye all: Yet in the Assembly **I had rather speak five words with my understanding**, that *by my voice* I might teach others also, **than ten thousand words in an *unknown* tongue**.

…Wherefore **tongues are for a sign**, not to them that believe, but **to them that believe not**: but prophesying *serves* not for them that believe not, but for them which believe.

…**If any man speak in an *unknown* tongue**, *let it be* by two, or at the most *by* three, and *that* by course; and **let one interpret**. But **if there be no interpreter, let him keep silence in the Assembly**

For the Mighty One is not *the author* of confusion, but of peace, as in all Assemblies of the saints.”

As can be seen in this passage is that the gift of speaking in “tongues” is not useful or edifying if there is no interpreter to explain what is being said. For this reason, Paul concludes the topic by stating that if there is no interpreter present, there should be no "tongues" spoken in the Assembly. What's more, he says that if there are more than three people doing it, it is confusion and therefore not of Yah.

Tithes

Technically, the first person in Scripture to tithe was Abraham.

Gen 14:14-20

> And when Abram heard that his brother was taken captive, **he armed** his trained *servants,* born in his own house, **three hundred and eighteen**, and **pursued** *them* unto Dan. And he divided himself against them, he and his servants, by night, and smote them, and **pursued** them unto Hobah, which *is* on the left hand of Damascus.
>
> And he brought back **all the goods**, and also brought again his brother Lot, and his goods, and the women also, and the people.
>
> ...And Melchizedek king of Salem brought forth bread and wine: and he *was* the priest of the most high Mighty One. And he blessed him, and said, Blessed *be* Abram of the most high Mighty One, possessor of heaven and earth: And blessed be the most high Mighty One, which **has delivered your enemies into your hand.**

And he gave him **tithes of all**.

Commenting on this account, the author of the book of
Hebrews summarizes in Heb 7:14, by saying:

> "Now consider how great this man *was*, unto whom
> even the patriarch Abraham gave the **tenth of the
> spoils**."

As can be observed, Abraham did not give a tenth of
everything he owned, or a tenth of everything he earned
throughout the year. Rather, he gave this divine Being a
tenth of the spoils of the battle he had just won.

The first person in Scripture to tithe his yearly income to
Yah was Jacob. The morning following his dream in Bethel
involving a latter and Yah's promise to bless all families of
the earth through his descendants, he made a vow to the
Mighty One.

Gen 28:20-22

> "...**If the Mighty One** will be with me, and will
> keep me in this way that I go, and **will give me
> bread to eat, and raiment to put on**, So that I
> come again to my father's house in peace; then shall
> Yah be my Mighty One: And this stone, which I
> have set *for* a pillar, shall be the Mighty One's
> house: and <u>of all that you shall give me</u> **I will
> surely give the tenth unto you**."

It is not revealed in Scripture how Jacob did this. To whom
did he directly give tithes too? It seems to be a mystery.
Nevertheless, from this point moving forward the principle

of tithing is established.

In giving the descendants of Jacob and those joined to them a moral code and judgments for the Promised Land they are getting ready to enter, Yah lays out three distinct tithes.

1st Tithe

Lev 27:30-33

> "And all the **tithe of the land**, *whether* of the **seed** of the land, *or* of the **fruit** of the tree, *is* Yah's: *it is* holy unto Yah. <u>And if a man will at all redeem *ought* of his tithes, he shall add thereto the fifth</u> *part* thereof. And concerning the tithe of the **herd**, or of the **flock**, *even* of whatsoever passes under the rod, <u>the tenth shall be holy unto Yah</u>. He shall not search whether it be good or bad, neither shall he change it: and if he change it at all, then both it and the change thereof shall be holy; it shall not be redeemed."

In this general tithe, a tenth of all increases ("income")—whether it be of fruit/grain of the land or sheep or goat of the flock, is set aside to give to Yah. And if it is redeemed, it is bought back for 120% of its value.

Deu 12:17-18

> "You may not eat within your gates **the tithe of your corn, or of your wine, or of your oil, or the firstlings of your herds or of your flock**, nor any of your vows which you vow, nor your freewill offerings, or heave offering of your hand:

But you must eat them before Yah your Mighty One **in the place which Yah your Mighty One shall choose**, you, <u>and your son, and your daughter, and your manservant, and your maidservant, and the Levite that *is* within your gates</u>: **and you shall rejoice** before Yah your Mighty One in all that you put your hands unto."

This tithe is eaten or given (if redeemed) at the place where Yah chose, along with everyone in one's household, including the Levite living within one's gates. It was a time of rejoicing.

2nd Tithe

Deu 14:22-27

"You shall truly **tithe all the increase** of your seed, that the field produces <u>year by year</u>. And you shall eat before Yah your Mighty One, <u>in the place which he shall choose to place his name there</u>, the **tithe** of your **corn**, of your **wine**, and of your **oil**, and the firstlings of your **herds** and of your **flocks**; that you may learn to fear Yah your Mighty One always. And if the way be too long for you, so that you are not able to carry it; *or* if the place be too far from you, which Yah your Mighty One shall choose to set his name there, when Yah your Mighty One has blessed you: Then shall you turn *it* into money, and bind up the money in your hand, and shall go unto the place which Yah your Mighty One shall choose: <u>And you shall bestow that money for whatsoever your soul lusts after, for oxen, or for sheep, or for wine, or for strong drink, or for</u>

whatsoever your soul desires: and **you shall eat there** before Yah your Mighty One, **and** you shall **rejoice**, you, <u>and your household</u>, <u>And the Levite</u> that *is* within your gates; you shall not forsake him; for he has no part nor inheritance with you."

Like the first tithe, this tithe was brought to the place where Yah chose and ate with one's household and the Levite within one's gates. It was also a time of rejoicing. However, this was only done once a year (v22).

Additionally, unlike the first tithe, this tithe could not be redeemed with money. Instead, if converted to money, it must be converted back into food and be eaten.

3rd Tithe

Deu 14:28-29

> **"At the end of three years** you shall bring all the **tithe of your increase the same year,** and shall lay *it* up within your gates: <u>And the Levite,</u> (because he has no part nor inheritance with you,) <u>and the stranger, and the fatherless, and the widow,</u> which *are* within your gates, <u>shall come, and shall eat and be satisfied"</u>

Deu 26:12

> "When you have made an end of tithing all the **tithes** of your **increase the third year,** *which is* the year of tithing, and have <u>given *it*</u> unto the Levite, the

stranger, the fatherless, and the widow, that they
may eat within your gates, and be filled;"

Amo 4:4

"Come to Bethel…and bring your slaughtering
every morning, *and* your **tithes after three years**:"

This tithe was unique in several ways. First, it was only
given in the third year for the increase of *that* year. Next, it
was given to the Levites, the stranger, the fatherless, and
the widow. It was not eaten by oneself and household.

Num 18:26-30

"Thus speak unto the Levites, and say unto them,
When ye take of the children of Israel the tithes
which I have given you from them for your
inheritance, then ye shall offer up an heave offering
of it for Yah, *even* a **tenth** *part* **of the tithe**. And
this your heave offering shall be reckoned unto you,
as though *it were* the corn of the threshingfloor, and
as the fulness of the winepress. Thus ye also shall
offer an heave offering unto Yah of all your tithes,
which ye receive of the children of Israel; and ye
shall give thereof Yah's heave offering to Aaron the
priest. Out of all your gifts ye shall offer every
heave offering of Yah, of all the best thereof, *even*
the hallowed part thereof out of it. Therefore you
shall say unto them, When ye have heaved the best
thereof from it, then it shall be counted unto the
Levites as the increase of the threshing floor, and as

the increase of the winepress. And <u>ye shall eat it in every place</u>, ye and your households: for <u>it *is* your reward for your service in the tabernacle</u> of the congregation."

This third tithe was given to the Levites, who would in turn, take a tenth (the best part) and give it to Aaron, the Cohen (Priest) as a "tithe of the tithe"—also called a "heave offering" (tribute). This tenth part was then piled up in the threshing floor—that is, a grain chamber, which was exclusively used by the Levites to eat as they serve in the tabernacle, and later the Temple.

Neh 12:44

> "And at that time were some appointed over the <u>chambers for the **treasures**</u>, for the offerings, for the first fruits, and **for the tithes**, to gather into them out of the fields of the cities the portions of the law **for the priests and Levites**"

The Hebrew word behind this word "treasures" is later translated as "storehouse" in Malachi 3:10:

> "Bring ye all the **tithes** into the **storehouse**, that there may be meat in mine house, and prove me now herewith, says Yah of hosts, if I will not open you the windows of heaven, and pour you out a blessing*"*

Of the three different Biblical tithes discussed, the third tithe, the tithe of the <u>third year</u>, is what the infamous Mal 3:8 is referring to. While this passage is all too often taken from its context by many "pastors" in order to coerce their congregation members to give their "church/ministry" a tenth of their income, the "New Testament" does no such thing.

In fact, the word *tithe* appears a total of <u>four</u> times in the "New Testament." One of these places, the tithe is specifically mentioned as going to the Levites (Heb 7:5).

The other <u>three</u> times the word is used, the act is part of hypocritical behavior.

Mat 23:23

> "Woe unto you, scribes and Pharisees, **hypocrites**! For ye pay **tithe**"

Luk 11:42

> "But woe unto you, **Pharisees**! For ye **tithe**"

Luk 18:11-12

> **The Pharisee** stood and prayed thus with himself, "Mighty One, I thank you, that I am not as other men *are,* extortioners, unjust, adulterers, or even as this publican. I fast twice in the week, I give **tithes** of all that I possess."

Please don't misunderstand me; tithing itself is not a bad thing. If the person tithing is doing so for the right reason—the reason the patriarch Jacob did it, they are doing an admirable thing.

However, if they choose not to tithe while there are no Temple services going on, they are certainly not "robbing Yah."

Furthermore, if one chooses to tithe, it should go toward sustaining the poor and vulnerable: particularly the qualified widow, the fatherless children and the alien (Deu 10:18, 14:29, 16:11, 14, 24:17-21, 26:12-13, Jer 7:6, 22:3, Zec 7:10).

Provision should also be provided for those who travel city to city (a house within one city to house within the next city) preaching the good news of repentance (Mat 10:10/Luk 10:7, 1Co 9:14). This provision should not be part of the voluntary tithe so as to avoid confusion by associating it with the tithe that was (and will again be) given to the Levites.

Chapter 11
Praise and Worship

Many of us have heard the phrase *praise and worship*. This phrase is often used in describing songs or the time at which when these songs are sung. Its own *genre*, a "praise and worship" song is thought of as a type of song that is sung corporately or individually to "praise" and "worship" the Almighty. The common assumption is that the words *praise* and *worship* mean the same thing.

However, when we look to Scripture and appropriate tools that bear out the original Hebrew and Aramaic words used, we can see that this is simply not true.

Worship

The primary Hebrew word for *worship* is שׁחה *shackah* (Strong's number H7812) meaning *bow down*, and is used 53 times in the Hebrew Scriptures. A few passages that show this meaning clearing within their context would be:

Gen 19:1

> ...and he bowed himself (H7812) <u>with his face toward the ground.</u>"

Exo 34:8

> And Moses...<u>bowed his head toward the earth</u>, and worshiped (H7812)

Num 22:31

> ...and he <u>bowed down his head,</u> and fell flat (H7812) on his face

Psa 22:9

> "All...shall...worship (H7812)...they...shall <u>bow (bend the knee)</u>"

Isa 49:23

> "..they shall <u>bow down</u> (H7812) to you with their <u>face toward the earth</u>"

Another Hebrew word that carries the same meaning as shachah is סגד sagad (Strong's' number H5456). A few passages to demonstrate would be

Isa 44:17

> "...he <u>fell down</u> (H5456) unto it, and worshiped (H7812) it"

Isa 44:15

> "...a mighty one, and worshiped (H7812) it...a graven image, and <u>fell down</u> (H5446) to it"

Isa 46:6

> "...they <u>fall down</u> (H5456), yea, they worship (H7812)."

This is the word used by Yeshua in John 4:23 when He said:

> "But the hour is coming, and now is, when the true worshippers (H5456) shall worship (H5456) the Father in spirit and in truth: for the Father seeks such to worship (H5456) him."

Here Yeshua makes it clear that our heavenly Father desires that we bow down to Him in a spiritual and true way. This entails "bowing" or bending the "knees" of our hearts, which is humbly submitting our desires to those of our Mighty One.

In other words, we must deny ourselves on a daily basis (Luk 9:23). In other words, we must circumcise our hearts (Deu 10:16). Meaning, cutting off the sinful nature we were all born with: selfishness and stubbornness (Col 2:11).

We must put His words in our hearts (Deu 6:6, 11:18, Psa 119:11) and learn to listen to His voice every single day; when we go to bed, when we awake, and all throughout the day (Deu 6:7).

Then we can know what it means to be a pleasing slaughtering to Him (Rom 12:1). The apostle Shaul made it clear that this is a daily lifestyle of dying to self (1 Cor 15:31, 2 Cor 4:16).

So the word *worship*, in the literal sense, means *bowing down*; and in the spiritual sense, means *submitting to His will daily*.

Praise

There are three primary Hebrew words for *praise*:

1) הלל *hallel* –used 77 times in the Hebrew Scriptures

2) ידה *yadah* –used 63 times in the Hebrew Scriptures

3) תהלה *tihilah* –used 51 times in the Hebrew Scriptures.

The word *hallel* is often used to suggest celebration or boasting. This term can also be used a negative way to refer to a foolish person who boasts in himself (Psa 5:5, 10:3, Isa 14:12). The word *hallelujah* is actually a phrase that uses this word and means *praise you Yah.*

Some notable Scripture references would be:

Gen 12:14-15

> And it came to pass, that, when Abram was come into Egypt, the Egyptians beheld the woman that she *was* very fair. The princes also of Pharaoh saw her, and **commended** (*hallel*) her before Pharaoh: and the woman was taken into Pharaoh's house.

1Ch 23:5

> Moreover four thousand *were* porters; and four thousand **praised** (*hallel*) Yah with the instruments which I made, *said David,* to praise *therewith.*

1Ch 23:28-30

> Because their office *was* to wait on the sons of Aaron for the service of the house of Yah…and to stand every morning to thank and **praise** *(hallel)* Yah, and likewise at even;

Psa 113:3

> "From the rising of the sun unto the going down of the same Yah's name *is* to be **praised** *(hallel).*"

Psa 119:164

> "Seven times a day do I **praise** *(hallel)* you because of your righteous judgments."

Psa 150:1-6

> "Praise you Yah. Praise the Mighty One in his sanctuary: **praise** him in the firmament of his power. **Praise** him for his mighty acts: **praise** him according to his excellent greatness. **Praise** him with the sound of the trumpet: **praise** him with the psaltery and harp. **Praise** him with the timbrel and dance: **praise** him with stringed instruments and organs. **Praise** him upon the loud cymbals: **praise** him upon the high sounding cymbals. Let everything that has breath **praise** Yah."

The word *yadah* is used more to describe someone using their hands in this action (the word for hand is *yad*). It is also the word that the name Yahudah, or "Judah" is named after. Interestingly enough, the word *yahah* can also mean *confess*—as in confess sins.

Some passages that use this word are:

Gen 29:35

> And she conceived again, and bare a son: and she said, "Now will I **praise** (yadah) Yah: therefore she called his name Judah; and left bearing."

Psa 92:1

> A Psalm *or* Song for the <u>Sabbath</u> day. "*It is a* good *thing* to give **thanks** (*yadah*) unto Yah, and to sing praises unto your name, O most High:"

Psa 118:29

> "O give **thanks** (*yadah*) unto Yah; for *he is* good: for his mercy *endures* forever."

Psa 119:62

> "At midnight I will rise to give **thanks** (*yadah*) unto you because of your righteous judgments."

The word *tihilah* specifically suggests singing songs. This word is where the name of all the Psalms (and the name of the book) comes from: *tehilim*.

Some passages that use this word are:

2Ch 20:22

> And when they began to <u>sing</u> and to **praise** (*tihilah*)

Neh 12:46

> … the singers, and <u>songs</u> of **praise** (*tihilah*) and
> thanksgiving unto Mighty One.

Psa 40:3

> "And he has put a new <u>song</u> in my mouth, *even*
> **praise** (*tihilah*) unto our Mighty One"

Psa 66:8

> "O bless our Mighty One, you people, and make the
> <u>voice</u> of his **praise** (*tihilah*) to be <u>heard</u>:"

Psa 149:1

> "…<u>Sing</u> unto Yah a new <u>song</u>, *and* his **praise**
> (*tihilah*) in the congregation of saints."

Thus, we can see that the word *worship* and the word
praise **do not** mean the same thing. While the word *praise*
is appropriate to use to describe singing songs to Yah, the
word *worship* is not. Worship is a lifestyle.

Chapter 12
Women in the Assembly

This chapter will be hard to accept by many. Some may just glance over it and label me a "chauvinist." However, I am simply the messenger delivering the message: the Word of Yah.

I believe the whole Bible (all 66 books) is inspired by the Spirit of Yah. This secular world and the powers thereof have had a great impact on the way we think as a society.

In this case, the feminist movement has actually undermined the way many believers understand the plain teachings of the Bible. We must remember Paul's warning in Romans 12:2: "be not conformed to this world."

This chapter, or the Scripture contained therein, **must not be twisted**. They are not saying that women are in any way inferior to men. Nor are do they give husbands any permission to neglect or abuse their wives. Rather, they are saying that women have special and unique roles to play in the Assembly and in their marriages.

That being said, the chapter will be divided into four sections: women teaching men in the Assembly, young women's responsibilities, older women's responsibilities, and wives.

Women teaching men in the Assembly:

1 Co 14:34-35

> "Let your women **keep silence in the assemblies**: for it **is not permitted unto them to speak**; but *they are commanded* to <u>be under obedience,</u> as also says the law. And if they will learn anything, **let them ask their husbands at home**: for it <u>is a shame for women to speak in the assembly</u>."

1 Ti 2:11-15

> "Let the woman **learn in silence** with all subjection. But **I suffer not a woman to teach, nor** to **usurp authority over the man**, but to **be in silence**. For Adam was first formed, then Eve. And Adam was not deceived, but the woman being deceived was in the transgression."

Young women's responsibilities:

1 Ti 2:9-10

> "In like manner also, that **women adorn themselves in modest apparel,** with shamefacedness and sobriety; **not with broided hair, or gold, or pearls, or costly array**; But (which becometh women professing godliness) with good works."

1 Ti 5:14

"I will therefore that **the younger women <u>marry</u>, bear children**, **guide the house**, <u>give none occasion to the adversary</u> to **speak reproachfully**."

1 Ti 2:15

"Notwithstanding she **shall be saved in childbearing**, if they continue in faith and charity and holiness with sobriety."

1 Co 11:5-6, 8-10

"But **<u>every</u> woman** <u>that prays or prophesy with *her* head uncovered</u> **dishonors her head**: for that is even all one **as if she were shaven. For if the woman be not covered, let her also be shorn**: but if it be a shame for a woman to be shorn or shaven, **let her [head also] be covered.**

For the man is not of the woman; but <u>the woman of the man</u>. Neither was the man created for the woman; but <u>the woman for the man</u>. **For this cause ought the woman to have authority on *her* head**"

Older women's responsibilities:

1 Co 11:5-6, 8-10

> "But <u>**every**</u> **woman** <u>that prays or prophesy with *her*</u>
> <u>head uncovered</u> **dishonors her head**: for that is
> even all one **as if she were shaven**. For **if the**
> **woman be not covered, let her also be shorn**: but
> if it be a shame for a woman to be shorn or shaven,
> **let her [head also] be covered**.
>
> For the man is not of the woman; but <u>the woman of</u>
> <u>the man</u>. Neither was the man created for the
> woman; but <u>the woman for the man</u>. **For this cause**
> **ought the woman to have authority on *her* head**"

Tit 2:3-5

> "The **aged women** likewise, that *they be* in
> behavior as becoming **holiness, not false accusers,**
> **not given to much wine**, teachers of good
> things; That **they may teach the young women** to
> be sober, to love their husbands, to love their
> children, *To be* discreet, chase, keepers at home,
> good, obedient to their own husbands, that the word
> of the Mighty One be not blasphemed."

Wives:

1 Co 11:3

"But I would have you know, that the head of every man is the Messiah; and **the head of the [wife]** *is* **the [husband]**; and the head of the Messiah *is* the Mighty One."

Tit 2:4-5

"…teach the young women to be sober, **love their husbands**, to **love their children**, *To be* **discreet, chase, keepers at home**, good, **obedient to their own husbands**, that the word of the Mighty One be not blasphemed."

Eph 5:22-24

"Wives, **submit yourselves** <u>unto your own husbands,</u> <u>as unto the Master.</u> For **the husband is the head of the wife**, even as the Messiah is the head of the Assembly: and He is the savior of the body. Therefore as the assembly is subject unto the Messiah, so *let* **the wives** *be* to their own **husbands** <u>in everything</u>."

Col 3:18

"Wives, **submit yourselves** <u>unto your own husbands,</u> as it is fit in the Master."

1 Ti 3:11

> "Even so [the servant's] wives[must] *be grave*, **not slanderers, sober, faithful** in all things."

1 Pe 3:1-6

> "Likewise, ye wives, *be* **in subjection** to your own husbands; that, if any obey not the word, they also may without the word be won by the conversation of the wives; While they behold **your chase conversation** *coupled* **with fear.**
>
> Whose adorning let it **not be that outward** *adorning* **of plaiting the hair,** and **of wearing of gold, or** of putting on of **apparel**; But *let it be* the hidden man of the heart, in that which is not corruptible, *even the ornament* of a **meek and quiet spirit**, which is in the sight of the Mighty One of great price. For **after this manner in the old time** the holy women also, who trusted in the Mighty One, adorned themselves, **being in subjection unto their own husbands:** Even as Sara **obeyed** Abraham, calling him master: whose daughters ye are, as long as ye do well."

Hopefully it can be seen that Yah's Word teaches:

> 1) **Women should not teach or usurp authority over men, but keep silent in the assembly** (1 Co 14:34-35 & 1 Ti 2:11-12), wearing head coverings to show their husband's authority over them (1 Co 11:5-6, 8-10).

2) **Young women should marry** (1 Ti 5:14), **have children** (1 Ti 5:14, 1 Ti 2:15, Tit 2:4), **be home-keepers** (Tit 2:5), **be obedient to their husbands** (1Co 14:34, Tit 2:5, 1 Pe 3:6), **submitting to his headship** (1 Co 11:3, Eph 5:22-24, Col 3:18) **even if he is not being obedient to Yah** (1 Pe 3:1).

3**) Older women should also be obedient to their husbands** (1 Co 14:34, 1 Pe 3:6**), submitting to his headship** (1 Co 11:3, Eph 5:22-24, Col 3:18), **even if he is not being obedient to Yah** (1Pe 3:1), **teaching the younger women to do the same** (Tit 2:4).

4) **All women should dress modestly** (1Ti 2:9-10, 1 Pe 3:3-4) **and have a meek and quiet spirit** (Tit 2:5, 1 Pe 3:4). Elsewhere, Yah also says that women should not wear articles of clothing, such as **pants**, that men wear (Deu 22:5). Women should dress like women; this means wearing long skirts or dresses that cover most of their legs, showing no cleavage, and not wearing form-fitting outfits.

It is the husband's responsibility to **love** and **cherish** his wife (Eph 5:25, Col 3:19, 1Pe 3:7) and **lead her** in Yah's instructions (1Co 11:3, 14:35) as well as **provide** for her and his children's physical needs (2Th 3:10).

If he is performing his responsibilities, and she hers, the marriage should not only last, but be **happy and fulfilling**.

And if it does not, remarriage to someone else (while both the man and the woman are still living) is not a legal option (Mar 10:6-12, Luk 16:18, Rom 7:2-3, 1 Co 7:10-11, 39).

This is not spelled out as concisely in the Hebrew Scriptures as it is the Aramaic. However, the Hebrew Scriptures teach that a marriage is a covenant before Yah (Pro 2:27, Mal 2:14), which implies that it is eternal. It also teaches that if we follow His example, we will not take another spouse even in the case of adultery (Eze 16:8,59-60, Jer 3:1,8,12-14, Hos 2:2,5,16-20). The Brenton (English translation of the Septuagint) of **Mal 2:14-16** spells out how Yah feels about divorce.

> "Yet ye said, 'Why?' Because Yah has borne witness **between you and the wife** of your youth, whom you have forsaken…the wife **of your covenant**.
>
> …But ye said, 'What does the Mighty One seek but a seed?' But take ye heed to your spirit, and **forsake not the wife of your youth**.
>
> But **if you should hate *your wife* and <u>put her away</u>**, says Yah the Mighty One of Israel, **then ungodliness shall cover your thoughts**, says Yah Almighty: therefore take ye heed to your spirit, and **forsake *them* not**."

The past is the past; we are responsible for our actions moving forward.

Chapter 13
Praying to the Father

In many ways, there is a disconnect between how modern day Christianity and "Messianic Judaism" does things and how the first century Assembly did things. This chapter addresses yet another example of this.

This chapter is not so much *how* we pray, but *who* we pray to. If one were to travel around to different prayer groups or Bible studies, they are likely to find people addressing their prayers to Yeshua. Many of these prayers may start off addressing the Father but at some point in the prayer the person praying switches over to start addressing Yeshua. Perhaps they do this intentionally; maybe not. Regardless, this practice of praying to Yeshua is becoming widespread.

In we look to the Aramaic Scriptures; however, we see no such practice. Instead, we see that prayers were addressed to Yah our Mighty One.

Rom 15:30

> "Now I beseech you, brethren, for the Master Yeshua the Messiah's sake…strive together with me in *your* **prayers to Mighty One for me**"

1Th 1:2

> "We **give thanks to the Mighty One** always for you all, making mention of you **in our prayers**"

Phi 1:4

> "I **thank my Mighty One**, making mention of you always **in my prayers**"

2Co 13:7

> "Now **I pray to the Mighty One** that ye do no evil"

Col 1:3

> "We **give thanks to the Mighty One** and the Father of our Master Yeshua...**praying** always for you"

Rev 8:4

> And the smoke of the incense, *which came* with the **prayers of the saints, ascended up before the Mighty One** out of the angel's hand.

In fact, Yeshua Himself taught us who to pray to:

Mat 6:9

> "After this manner therefore **pray ye**: '*Our **Father**'*"

Joh 16:26-27

> "At that day ye shall **ask in my name**: and I say **not**

unto you, **that I will pray the Father for you**: For **the Father himself** loves you, because ye have loved me, and have believed that I came out from the Mighty One."

What is the difference between praying to the Father and praying to Yeshua; are not they the same Being?

Scripture teaches quite the opposite.

Mat 19:16-17

> And behold, one came and said unto Him, "Good Master"
>
> …And He [Yeshua] said unto him, **"Why call** you **me good?** There is **none good but** One, that is, the **Mighty One**"

Joh 17:3

> "And this is life eternal: that they might know **You, the only** true **Mighty One**, <u>and</u> Yeshua the Messiah whom You have sent."

Joh 20:17

> Yeshua said unto her, "…go to My brethren and say unto them, 'I ascend unto My Father and your Father, and **to My Mighty One** and your Mighty One.'"

1 Cor 8:6

> "yet to us there is but **one Mighty One**, the Father, from whom are all things, and we in Him, <u>and</u> **one Master Yeshua the Messiah**"

Eph 4:5-6

> "one Master [Yeshua], one faith, one baptism, **one Mighty One and Father of all**, who is above of all, and through all."

1 Tim 2:5

> "For there is **one Mighty One** <u>and</u> one mediator between Mighty One and men, the man **Yeshua the Messiah.**"

Act 10:38

> "How the **Mighty One** anointed Yeshua…who went about doing good… for **the Mighty One was with him**."

Rom 1:7

> "…Grace to you and peace from **the Mighty One our Father** <u>and</u> the Master Yeshua the Messiah."

Rom 15:6

> "…that ye may…glorify **the Mighty One, even the Father of** our Master **Yeshua** the Messiah."

1Co1:4

> "Grace be unto you and peace from **the Mighty One our Father** <u>and</u> from the Master Yeshua the Messiah."

2Co 1:2

> "Grace be to you and peace from **the Mighty One our Father**, <u>and</u> from…Yeshua"

2 Cor 11:32

> **"The Mighty One and Father of** our Master **Yeshua** the Messiah"

Gal 1:1

> "Paul, an apostle (not of men, neither by man, but by Yeshua the Messiah <u>and</u> **the Mighty One** the Father, **who raised Him** from the dead),"

Gal 1:3

> "Grace be to you and peace <u>from</u> **the Mighty One the Father** <u>and from</u> our Master Yeshua the Messiah,"

Eph 1:2

> "Grace be to you and peace <u>from</u> **the Mighty One our Father** <u>and from</u> the Master Yeshua the Messiah."

Eph 1:3

"Blessed be **the Mighty One and Father of** our
Master **Yeshua** the Messiah, who has blessed us
with all spiritual blessings"

Eph 1:17

"I pray that **the Mighty One of our Master
Yeshua** the Messiah…may give unto you the
spirit of wisdom and revelation"

Eph 6:13

"Peace be to the brethren, and love with faith, from
the Mighty One the Father <u>and</u> the Master Yeshua
the Messiah."

Phi 1:2

"Grace be unto you and peace <u>from</u> **the
Mighty One our Father** <u>and from</u> the Master
Yeshua the Messiah."

Col 1:2

"…Grace be unto you and peace from **the
Mighty One our Father** <u>and</u> the Master Yeshua
the Messiah."

Col 1:3

"We give thanks to **the Mighty One and the
Father of** our Master Yeshua the Messiah"

1 Th 1:1

> "...Unto the assembly of the Thessalonians which is <u>in</u> **the Mighty One the Father** <u>and in</u> the Master Yeshua the Messiah"

2 Th 1:2

> "Grace unto you and peace from **the Mighty One our Father** <u>and</u> the Master Yeshua"

1 Tim 1:2

> "...Grace, mercy, and peace from **the Mighty One our Father** <u>and</u> Yeshua the Messiah our Master."

2 Tim 1:2

> "... Grace, mercy, and peace from **the Mighty One the Father** <u>and</u> the Messiah Yeshua our Master."

Tit 1:4

> "...Grace, mercy, and peace from **the Mighty One the Father** <u>and</u> the Master Yeshua the Messiah our Savior."

Phi 1:3

> "Grace to you and peace from **the Mighty One our Father** <u>and</u> the Master Yeshua the Messiah."

1 Pe 1:3

> "Blessed be **the Mighty One and Father of our** Master **Yeshua** the Messiah"

2 Jo 1:3

> "Grace, mercy, and peace be with you from **the Mighty One the Father** and from the Master Yeshua the Messiah, the Son of the Father"

Jud 1:1

> "…To those who are sanctified by **the Mighty One the Father**, <u>and</u> preserved in Yeshua"

Joh 8:42

> Yeshua said unto them, "…**I proceeded** forth and came **<u>from</u>** (G1537) **the Mighty One**; neither came I of Myself, but He sent Me."

To get a better idea as to what it means that Yeshua came *from* Yah, let us take note to how this Greek word is used in the "Gospels." (The Greek was translated directly from the original Aramaic.)

Mat 1:3
> "And Judas begat Phares…**of (G1537)** Thamar"

Mat 1:5

> "And Salmon begat Booz **of (G1537)** Rachab; and Booz begat Obed **of (G1537)** Ruth"

Mat 1:6

> "And Jesse begat David the king; and David the
> king begat Solomon **of (G1537)**...*the wife* of Urias"

This is critical, because it contradicts the idea that Yeshua
is eternal. While Yah had no origin as He always existed,
Yeshua did: His father, Yah, the Mighty One. John 8:42,
16:27 & 17:8 are not the only verses that say this either.

Psa 2:7

> "...Yah has said unto me, You *art* my Son; this day
> have **I begotten you**."

Yah has never been "begotten." Nobody brought Him forth.
However, Yeshua has been; by Yah, His father and
originator.

Heb 1:6

> "And again, when **he bring in the first begotten
> into the world**, he said, 'And let all the angels of
> the Mighty One worship him.'"

This phrase "let all the angels of the Mighty One worship
Him" comes from the original reading (LXX and Aramaic
Peshitta) of Deu 32:43. This was said long before Mary
conceived Yeshua. So at some point, long before Yeshua
was born of Mary, Yah brought Him into the world.

Rev 3:14

> "...These things says the Amen...the **beginning of the creation of the Mighty One**"

Here it says that Yeshua is the beginning of Yah's creation. Pair this up with the following Scriptures and we are taught that He was created before anything else and is the instrument Yah used to create the world.

Heb 1:2

> "...has in these last days spoken to us by [Yeshua]...through whom also **He made the ages**,"

Eph 3:9

> "...**the Mighty One who created** all through Yeshua the Messiah."

1Co 8:6

> "for us there is one Mighty One, the Father, *from whom all* came and for whom we *live, and one Master Yeshua the Messiah, through* whom all came"

Once again, all things—including Yeshua, came *from* Yah, the Mighty One, while all things came *through* Yeshua, the Word of Yah.

The first couple verses of John do not say anything to the contrary.

Joh 1:1-3

> "In the beginning was the Word, and the Word *was with* the Mighty One, and the Word *was* the Mighty One. The same was in the beginning with the Mighty One. All came to be *through* (G1223) [Yeshua], and without Him not even one came to be that came to be."

Yeshua not only existed before the world was created, but He represents the Word of Yah (Psa 33:6, 9, Heb 11:3) and therefore Yah Himself. After all, Yah's Word can be viewed as an extension of Himself. When we obey Yah's Word, we obey Yah.

Furthermore, Yeshua is called both 'Yah' and the 'Mighty One' a few times in Scripture because He represents Yah the Mighty One. (For this reason He is also called Israel. See Isa 49:3 & Hos 11:1). (Similarly, angels are referred to as Yah the Mighty One. See Gen 32:30/Hos 12:4, Jdg 13:21-22, & Zec 3:1-2/Jud 1:9, etc.)

Also, once Exo 3:15 is translated correctly one can see that Yeshua never claimed to be Yah, He who *will be*. The LXX of Exo 3:15 and the Greek of Joh 8:58 also bear this out.

Furthermore, most English translations correctly understand the supposed "I AM" statement made by Yeshua in Joh 8:23-24 as *I am he*. He was claiming to be the Messiah, Yah's Son whom He sent to earth. The Pharisees didn't want to accept that He was the Messiah, the Son of Yah. See also John 10:33-38.

If it **appears** that _one_ passage of Scripture contradicts _thirty_, then it is time to reevaluate how _we_ understand that _one_ passage.

The truth is, that just as a wife is **one** with her husband (Gen 2:24, Mat 19:5) and submits to him (Eph 5:22-24, Col 3:18 , 1Co 14:34, Tit 2:5, 1Pe 3:6), and we can be **one** with Yeshua (Joh 17:11 & 21-23) and submit to Him (Luk 6:46, 17:10, 1Co 3:23, Eph 5:24), Yeshua is **one** with His Father, Yah the Mighty One (Joh 10:30, 14:9, 20:28) and submits to Him (Luk 22:42, Joh 15:10, 1Co 3:23).

1Co 11:3

> "...**the head** of every man is the Messiah;
> and **the head** of the woman *is* the man;
> and **the head** of the Messiah *is* the Mighty One."

Not only do we pray to Yah our Mighty One and Father because Yeshua tells us to, but because in the end, He is the One who everything goes to.

1Co 15:28

> "And when all things shall be subdued unto [Yeshua], then shall the **Son also himself be subject unto [Yah]** that put all things under Him, that the Mighty One may be all in all."

Chapter 14
Fellowship Not Church

There is quite a difference between the modern understanding of the word *church* and the Biblical concept of the Hebrew word *qahal* and the corresponding Greek word *ekklesia*. This chapter will seek to highlight this difference.

First, let us look at the words *qahal/ekklesia.*

Act 7:38

> "This is he [Moses] that was in the *ekklesia* in the wilderness with the angel which speak to him **in the mount Sina,** and *with* our fathers: who **received the lively oracles** to give unto us:"

Deu 4:10

> "*Especially* the day that you stood before Yah your Mighty One **in Horeb**, when Yah said unto me, Gather me the people together (*qahal)*, and I will make them **hear my words**"

Here we can see that the event spoken of in Acts 7 and the event spoken of in Deuteronomy 4 are this same event. Mount Sinai, in Horeb, was where the people were gathered together to receive the living words of Yah.

Therefore, we can see that the Biblical word that has been translated *church* refers to Yah's people gathered together.

This is the purpose of fellowship. Coming together **as one** body in His name!

As David so beautifully put it in Psalms 133:1

> "Behold, how good and how pleasant *it is* for brethren to dwell together **in unity**!"

This unification is strongly encouraged in the Aramaic Scriptures:

Rom 15:6

> "That ye may **with one mind** *and* one mouth glorify the Mighty One, even the Father of our Master Yeshua the Messiah."

2Co 13:11

> "Finally, brethren…be **of one mind**…and the Mighty One of love and peace shall be with you."

Php 1:27

> "… stand fast in one spirit, **with one mind** striving **together** for the faith of the gospel;"

Php 2:2

> "Fulfill ye my joy, that ye be likeminded, having the same love, *being* of one accord, **of one mind**."

1Pe 3:8

> "Finally, *be ye* all **of one mind**, having compassion one of another"

Why is fellowship necessary?

Heb 10:25

> "Not forsaking the assembling of ourselves together, as the manner of some *is;* but **exhorting [comforting]** *one another:* and so much the more, as ye see the Day approaching."

1Th 5:11

> "Wherefore **comfort yourselves** together, and **edify one another**, even as also ye do."

Fellowship is beneficial for us: we all need encouragement. (This encouragement comes from each other, not from the person on the pulpit.)

Heb 13:16 (YLT)

> "…of fellowship, be not forgetful, for with such slaughtering **the Mighty One is well-pleased**."

Fellowship is also one of the ways we please Yah.

We must come together as believers **on a regular basis**.

Thousands of years ago, Yah commanded us to call set-apart gatherings **weekly** and on seven appointed days **annually**.

Lev 23:2-3, 6-8, 15, 21, 24, 27, 34-36

> "Speak unto the children of Israel, and say unto them, *Concerning* the appointed times of Yah, which **ye shall proclaim** *to be* **set-apart convocations**, *even* these *are* my appointed times.

Weekly

Six days shall work be done: but the **seventh day** *is* the Sabbath of rest, **an set-apart convocation**; ye shall do no work *therein:* it *is* <u>the Sabbath</u> of Yah in all your dwellings.

Yearly

1st

And on the <u>fifteenth day of the [first] month</u> *is* the feast of unleavened bread unto Yah: seven days ye must eat unleavened bread. **In the first day ye shall have an set-apart convocation**: ye shall do no servile work therein

2nd

in the seventh day *is* **an set-apart convocation**: ye shall do no servile work *therein.*

3rd

And ye shall count unto you from the morrow after the Sabbath, <u>from the day that ye brought the sheaf of the wave offering; seven Sabbaths shall be complete</u>…And **ye shall proclaim on the selfsame day, *that* it may be an set-apart convocation unto you:** ye shall do no servile work *therein: it shall be* a statute forever in all your dwellings throughout your generations.

4th

Speak unto the children of Israel, saying<u>, In the seventh month, in the first *day* of the month,</u> **shall ye have** a rest day, a memorial of blowing of trumpets, **an set-apart convocation**.

5th

Also <u>on the tenth *day* of this seventh month</u> *there shall be* a day of atonement: **it shall be an set-apart convocation unto you**; and ye shall afflict your souls

6th

Speak unto the children of Israel, saying, <u>The fifteenth day of this seventh month</u> *shall be* the feast of tabernacles *for* seven days unto Yah. **On the first day** *shall be* **an set-apart convocation:** ye shall do no servile work *therein.*

7th

Seven days ye shall offer an offering made by fire unto Yah: <u>on the eighth day</u> **shall be an set-apart convocation unto you**; and ye shall offer an offering made by fire unto Yah: it *is* a solemn assembly; *and* ye shall do no servile work *therein.*"

In total, there are 59 days out of the year we are commanded to come together in fellowship (52 weekly Sabbaths and 7 annual rest-days). (Yom Kippur is the Sabbath of the 7 annual rest-days.)

In addition to this, coming together more often is not a bad practice (Act 2:46, 5:42).

Although there is nothing wrong with assembling in a building, the point of fellowship is not to go to a building. The point of fellowship is assembling together.

We can look to the first century Assembly and see the example they left us. They met in each other's homes.

Acts 2:46

> And they, continuing daily with one accord in the temple, and breaking bread from **house to house**

Acts 5:42

> And daily in the temple, and **in every house**, they ceased not to teach and preach Yeshua the Messiah.

Acts 8:3

> As for Saul, he made havoc of the assembly, entering into **every house**

Acts 12:12

> ...he came to **the house** of Mary...where many were gathered together praying.

Acts 20:20

"And how I...have taught you publicly, and
from **house to house**"

This Biblical concept seems to be completely foreign to
much of Evangelical Christianity today. In the age of the
"Megachurch," one is left to wonder when the intimacy and
interpersonal edification of fellowship became a business.

Take, for example, two of the largest megachurches in
America. Just five miles apart from one another, over $135
million was collectively spent on the buildings alone. (One
is former NBA stadium). Their **annual** budgets are a
combined $126 million. This is just 2 of over 1,300
megachurches in the U.S. alone. This is in addition to the
3,000 plus Catholic parishes in this country; that, by the
numbers qualify to be considered megachurches.

Sufficed to say, something doesn't add up.

The "gospel" should not be sold to make a profit (Mat 10:8,
1 Co 9:6, 2 Co 6:4, 1 Ti 3:3 & 3:8, Tit 1:7, 1 Pe 5:2, 2 Pe
2:3).

Chapter 15
Keeping Torah

Torah is the Hebrew word that is translated as "law." The word itself literally means *instruction*. This word can refer to the five books attributed to Moses (Luk 24:44, Acts 28:23), or to all the Scriptures (Zec 7:12, Joh 10:34, 15:25).

As renewed covenant believers, how do we know what parts of the "***Mosaic*** Torah" are <u>not</u> applicable to us?

Yeshua made several statements that <u>none</u> of the Words His Father gave His people are obsolete.

Mat 4:4/Luk 4:4

> But He [Yeshua] answered and said, "It is written, **Man shall** not **live by** bread alone, but by <u>**every word that proceeds out of the mouth of Yah**</u>."

Mat 5:17-19

> **"Think not that I am come to destroy the law**, or the prophets: I am not come to destroy, but to fulfil. For verily I say unto you, <u>**Till heaven and earth pass, one jot or one tittle shall in no wise pass**</u> **from the law**, till all be fulfilled. Whosoever therefore shall break **one of these <u>least commandments</u>**, and shall teach men so, he shall be called the least in the kingdom of heaven: but whosoever shall **do and teach *them***, the same shall be called great in the kingdom of heaven."

Luk 16:17

> "And it is easier for **heaven and earth to pass**, than **one tittle** of the **law** to fail."

Mat 23:2-3a, 23:23

> "The scribes and the Pharisees sit in **Moses'** seat: All therefore **whatsoever** [he] bid you observe, *that* **observe and do**"

> …the weightier *matters* of **the law**, judgment, mercy, and faith: these **ought ye to have done**, and **not to leave the other undone**."

That being said, it can be observed that some parts of five books of Moses were either **1)** only meant to last for a limited amount of time, or **2)** can only be applied to ancient Israel while living in the Promised Land with the appointed judges.

A couple examples of these to two types of decrees are:

> *1) "You shall not allow a dismembered male, a child born of sexual immorality, an Ammonite or a Moabite up to the 10th generation become part of the assembly of Yah"* –Due 23:1-3

> *2) "Eye for eye, tooth for tooth, hand for hand, foot for foot, burning for burning, wound for wound, stripe for stripe"* –Exo 21:24-25

1) For the first example, the commands give an expiration date within them. We can be certain that this was only for the first 10 generations of Ammonites and Moabites from the time the decree was given and not meant to be taken as a perpetual decree because King David was a 4th generation Moabite.

There was no such thing as a 10th generation Moabite from ones father's side. If a Moabite joins himself to the tribes of Israel, he is no longer considered a Moabite.

For example, Caleb, the son of Jephunneh (1Ch 4:15), was apparently adopted by Kenaz (1Ch 4:13, Jos 15:17/Jdg 1:13), which gave him the right to belong to the tribe of Judah (Jos 15:13). Instead of belonging to the "mixed multitude" (Exo 12:38), he is said to come from the tribe of Judah (Num 13:6, 34:19).

Thus, the convert's male descendants would not be considered Moabites either. For this reason, a 10th generation Moabite would only work if a <u>Moabite woman married a male Israelite</u>. Their great-great-great-great-great-great-great grandson would be a 10th generation Moabite. See also Ezr 9:1-2.

David, although within the 10 generations, was clearly allowed in the assembly of Yah and was even appointed king. For further verification, see also Isa 56:3-5.

It is not too difficult to understand that there was some reason Yah gave such decrees. They must have served a purpose.

2) In the second example, the decree is called a "judgment" (Exo 21:1). These "judgments" were the **judicial system of the Land**. This word "judgment" comes from the Hebrew word *mishpat* (H4941 in the Strong's concordance). The Lexicon to the Biblical Hebrew for this has:

> *judgment, justice, ordinance:*
>
> > *1) act of <u>deciding a case</u>*
> > *2) place, <u>court</u>, <u>seat of judgment</u>*
> > *3)process, procedure, litigation (<u>before judges</u>)*
> > *4) <u>case</u>, cause (presented for judgment)*
> > *5) <u>sentence</u>, decision (of judgment)*
> > *6) execution (of judgment)*

Ever since we have been out of the land and without judges in place, these judgments can no longer be enforced. Furthermore, we live under the jurisdictions of the respective countries in which we live and are subjects to.

In the United States, for instance, there is a similar judgment that says if someone is convicted of ***murder***, that person is either sentenced to life in prison or ***death*** by the electric chair or lethal injection: *"life for life"* (Deu 19:21).

These ancient Judgments maintained justice for the ancient Israelites and acted as their judicial system.

Deu 1:16-17

> "And I charged your **judges** at that time, saying,
> Hear *the causes* between your brethren, and **judge**

righteously between *every* man…Ye shall not respect persons **in judgment;**"

Deu 4:5, 14

"Behold, I have taught you statutes and **judgments**, even as Yah my Mighty One commanded me, that **ye should do so in the [promised] land**

And Yah commanded me at that time to teach you statutes and **judgments**, that **ye might do them in the land** where ye go over to possess it."

Deu 5:31

"…the **judgments**, which you shall teach them, that **they may do *them* in the [promised] land**"

Deu 6:1

"Now these *are* the…the **judgments**…that ye might **do *them* in the land** where ye go to possess"

Deu 12:1

"These *are* the statutes and **judgments**, which **ye shall observe to do in the [promised] land**,"

While as a whole, this judicial system was about maintaining justice, there were certain instances in these *laws of the land* where justice was diminished.

Some examples of judgments for the ancient Land of Israel that actually took away justice include:

- allowing murder in certain circumstances (Exo 21:13/Num 35:11-15, 26-27)

- allowing the ownership and ruling over other people (Lev 25:44-46)

- treating a slave's life as less valuable than a non-slave's life (Exo 21:20,12)

- allowing a man to defile a virgin or bribe her father for his consent to marry (Exo 22:16-17, Deu 22:29)

- allowing divorce and polygamy (unfair to the first wife if she is divorced in favor of a newer wife) (Deu 24:1, Exo 21:10, Deu 21:15-17)

In all these cases, the judgments for ancient Israel were suitable for their time. However, when Yeshua returns and re-establishes the Kingdom of the Mighty One on earth (1 Cor 15:23-25, 2 Tim 4:1, Isa 9:7/Dan 7:13-14/Rev 12:10/20:4&6), it is likely He will update such judgments.

After all, **He will judge with equity** (Psa 98:9, Isa 11:4, 42:1, Mic 4:3, Mat 12:18).

He is anti-divorce (Mat 5:32/Mar 10:5-12/Mat 19:4-9). He is also against taking revenge (Mat 5:39, 26:52, Pro 20:22). He is also anti-polygamy (Mat 19:4-5/Mar 10:6-8). The same could be said for the other examples given.

However, all the decrees that are not called "*judgments*," or that are not identifiable as self-expiring, are applicable to Yah's people **no matter where or when we live.**

These laws include:

- laws about **idolatry** and **sexual immorality** (omitting the death penalty*)

- laws about "**holy**" **days** (omitting animal slaughtering done by Levites, traveling to one location and the death penalty*)

- laws about **circumcision** and **redemption of the first born son**

- laws about **rearing children** after His way

- **dietary** laws

- all other laws about **"holiness"** and our relationship with Yah**

    Until Yeshua returns. At this time, the Levitical priesthood will resume (Mal 3:3, Hos 3:4-5). Thus, at this time, tithes will resume, as well as animal slaughtering, Temple service, and the three annual pilgrimages. The years of rest/release, the Jubilee years, and the agricultural laws will also resume at this time.

These laws are **eternal expectations** Yah has for those in a covenant relationship with Him.

There is no need for *"picking and choosing."*

Mark 7: Traditions or Torah?

In Mar 7:19, it is written:

> "because it doth not enter into his heart, but into the belly, and into the drain it doth go out, **purifying all the meats**."

Some would argue, based on this verse that the Messiah is saying that the Torah requirement forbidding the eating of certain meats is no longer something Yah asks of us.

I would question this understanding and instead seek to understand this verse in its context, Mark chapter 7.

> And gathered together unto him are **the Pharisees**, and certain of the scribes, having come from Jerusalem, and having seen certain of his disciples with <u>defiled hands</u>--that is, unwashed--eating bread, they found fault; for **the Pharisees**, and all the Judeans, <u>if they do not wash the hands to the wrist, do not eat</u>, holding the **tradition of the elders**, and, *coming* from the market-place, if they do not baptize themselves, they do not eat; and many other things there are that they received to hold, baptisms of cups, and pots, and brazen vessels, and couches.

> Then question him do **the Pharisees** and the scribes, `Wherefore do your disciples not walk

according to the **tradition of the elders**, but with
unwashed hands do eat the bread?' and he
answering said to them--`Well did Isaiah prophesy
concerning you, hypocrites, as it has been written,
This people with the lips doth honor Me, and their
heart is far from Me; and in vain do they worship
Me, teaching teachings, commands of men; for,
having put away the [Torah], ye hold the **tradition
of men**, baptisms of pots and cups; and many other
such like things ye do.'

And he said to them, "Well do ye put away the
[Torah] that **your tradition** ye may keep; for Moses
said, 'Honor your father and your mother; and, He
who is speaking evil of father or mother--let him die
the death' (Exo 20:12 & 21:17); and ye say, 'If a
man may say to father or to mother, Korban (that is,
a gift), *is* whatever you may be profited out of
mine,' and no more do ye suffer him to do anything
for his father or for his mother, setting aside the
word of the Mighty One for **your tradition** that ye
delivered; and many such like things ye do."

And having called near all the multitude, he said to
them, "Hearken to me, ye all, and understand; there
is nothing from without the man entering into him
that is able to defile him, but the things coming out
from him, those are the things defiling the man. If
any has ears to hear--let him hear."

And when he entered into a house from the
multitude, his disciples were questioning him about
the simile, and he says to them, "So also ye are
without understanding! Do ye not perceive that
nothing from without entering into the man is able
to defile him? because it doth not enter into his
heart, but into the belly, and into the drain it doth

go out, purifying all the meats."

And he said—"That which is coming out from the man, that doth defile the man; for from within, out of the heart of men, the evil reasoning do come forth, adulteries, whoredom, murders, thefts, covetous desires, wickedness, deceit, arrogance, an evil eye, evil speaking, pride, foolishness; all these evils do come forth from within, and they defile the man."

The idea that not washing your hands before eating is eating with defiled hands (7:2) and is therefore eating defiled food (7:15, 7:18, 7:20 & 7:23), was a tradition of the Jewish authorities in the first century—namely the Pharisees (7:1, 7:3 & 7:5).

In fact, this tradition lives on today within Judaism.

The fact that this was a man-made tradition is confirmed in 7:3, 7:5, 7:8, 7:9, & 7:13.

The fact that this man-made tradition contradicts Torah is confirmed in 7:8, 7:9 & 7:13.

So in 7:19, is the Messiah taking issue with the Torah regarding clean and unclean animals, or the man-made tradition of washing your hands prior to eating so as not to defile it?

The parallel account of this story is found in Mat 15:1-20. At the end of this account, the Messiah says:

"These defile the man, <u>but to eat with unwashed hands does not defile the man.</u>"

Acts 15: Traditions or Torah?

As previously established, the Jewish authorities of the first century—namely the Pharisees, had their own laws that they were subjecting the people to. They taught the people to obey their "commands of men" (Mat 15:9/Mar 7:7). These commands included more than just washing hands (Mar 7:13).

Among these commands was an ultra-strictness regarding the Sabbath (Mat 12:2/Mar 2:24/Luk 6:2, Mat 12:10/Mar 3:2/Luk6:7, Joh 5:10, etc.). In fact, the Pharisees accused the Messiah of breaking the Sabbath (Joh 5:18 & Joh 9:16). In order for the Messiah to be the perfect Lamb of Yah, he must have been sinless (1 Pe 2:22, 1 Jo 3:5, 2 Co 5: 21).

Although the Pharisees accused the Messiah of sinning, He did not. Therefore, we know that the Pharisees were adding their own (man-made) laws to the Torah regarding the Sabbath. They were making it a burden.

This is why the Messiah said that the Sabbath is made for man—that is, it's a blessing; not man for the Sabbath. The Sabbath, or any other command of Yah, should not be a burden. But adding a multitude of man-made laws to Yah's laws was, and is, making them nearly impossible to obey. It is placing a "yoke" on the necks of the people. In Mat 23:4, speaking of the Pharisees, the Messiah said:

> "For they bind heavy burdens, **hard to bear**, and lay
> them on men's shoulders, but with their finger they do
> not wish to move them."

This is why, in response the believing Pharisees (Act 15:5),
Simon Peter said in verse 10:

> "Now then, why do you try the Mighty One by putting
> a yoke on the neck of the disciples which neither our
> fathers **nor we were able to bear**?"

Galatians: Traditions or Torah?

Saul (aka Paul) begins his letter to the believers in Galatia
by speaking of the "Gospel"-that is the Good News of the
Messiah (Gal 1:11):

> "And I make known to you, brothers, that the
> Gospel announced by me is **not according
> to man**."

He then immediately addresses his former way of life
within Judaism (Gal 1:14):

> "And I progressed in Judaism beyond many of my
> age in my race, being more exceedingly zealous for
> the **traditions** of my fathers."

Speaking of the same believers of Acts 15:5, he writes (Gal
2:4):

"But as for the false brothers, snakingly brought in, who sneaked in to spy out our freedom which we have in the Messiah Yeshua in order to **enslave us**, to these we did not yield in subjection, not even for an hour, so that the truth of the Good News remains with you."

He then cites an example of Simon Peter's misunderstanding (as is also recorded in Acts 10:10-17; 28) in holding to the man-made law that Jews cannot associate with Gentiles (Gal 2:11-14):

"And when Peter came to Antioch, to the face I stood up against him, because he was blameworthy, for before the coming of certain from James, with the nations he was eating, and when they came, **he was withdrawing and separating himself**, fearing those of the circumcision, and dissemble with him also did the other Jews, so that also Barnabas was carried away by their dissimulation. But when I saw that they are not walking uprightly to the truth of the good news, I said to Peter before all, `If you, being a Jew, in the manner of the nations do live, and not in the manner of the [Pharisaic] Jews, how the nations do you **compel to live as [Pharisaic] Jews**"

He then speaks of the faith spoken of in the Torah, as opposed to the works thereof, void of faith. (This theme of his is in many of his other letters, encapsulated precisely in Romans 9:31-32.) This is why he uses the peculiar phrase in Gal 2:19:

"For through the law, I died to the law"

What he is saying here is that through the law of Yah, he is dead to the laws of man. He elsewhere (Rom 6:1-8:13, for example) explains that the laws of man—i.e. that of the flesh, is also called the law of sin and death. But in his letter to the Galatians, he is not getting into this additional explanation. Rather, he is speaking of the man-made laws imposed on believers from those of the religion of which he came out. This is confirmed again in the ending of his letter

Gal 6:12-15:

> "As many as wish to make a good show in the flesh, these **compel you to [live as Pharisaic Jews]**, only so that they should not be persecuted for the *stauros* of the Messiah. For [the Pharisees] do not even watch over the Torah, but they wish to have you circumcised so that they might boast in your flesh. And for me, let it not be that I should boast except in the *stauros* of our Master Yeshua the Messiah, through whom the world has been impaled to me, and I to the world. For in the Messiah Yeshua neither [Jew] nor [Gentile] has any strength, but a renewed creature."

The fact that Paul was addressing the rabbinic, man-made traditions is evident in such passages as Titus 1:13-14:

> "This witness is true. Wherefore rebuke them sharply, that they may be sound in the faith; **Not giving heed to Jewish** fables, and **commandments of men**, that turn from the truth."

And Colossians 2:8-22:

> "Beware lest any man spoil you through philosophy and vain deceit, after the **tradition of men**, after the

rudiments of the world, and not after the Messiah…blotting out the handwriting of ordinances that was against us, which was contrary to us, and took it out of the way, nailing it to his *stauros*…Which all are to perish with the using; after **the commandments** and doctrines **of men**."

Paul Misunderstood

What needs to be understood about Paul's letters is that they are hard to comprehend. If we do not have a solid foundation, laid out in the previous Scriptures, we can easily mistake Paul's letters as to be encouraging lawlessness:

2 Pe 3:16-17

"…[Paul's] letters contain some things that are hard to understand, which ignorant and unstable people distort… to their own destruction. Therefore, dear friends, since you have been forewarned, be on your guard so that you may not be carried away by the error the lawless"

Saul himself was aware that his letters were being misunderstood:

"And not *rather*, (as we be slanderously reported, and as some affirm that we say,) 'Let us do evil (sin), that good (grace) may come'" (Rom 3:8)

and

"What then? Shall we sin (be disobedient to Yah's law), because we are not under the law, but under grace? The Mighty One forbids!" (Rom 6:15)

Being "under the law" and being of "works of the law" are different ways of saying being "religious" without truly putting our trust and hope in Yah. It is thinking that we can be "right with Yah" by our own merits; like we can be declared righteous by doing good things. In the first century, this was what the vast majority of the Pharisees were doing. Today, this is what many Christians (Catholics and Protestants) do.

They follow the "rules" such as tithing and church attendance, as if simply going through the motions could make a person "right with Yah." They follow man-made traditions such as the Sacraments (in the case of Catholics) or baptism and weekly communion (in the case of most Protestants). These things are not bad things to do. It's just that these things, and others, are in many cases treated as necessities to becoming and/or maintaining a "Christian" status; thus ensuring a good standing in Yah's eyes.

There are many Biblical examples of people who obeyed the Torah, but were not "under the law" or of "works of the law." Such examples include:

Moses, Joshua, Celeb, Esther, Ruth, David, Solomon, Josiah, Jeremiah, Isaiah, Ezekiel, Danial, Yeshua, Simon Peter, and Paul, to name a few.

Let us follow the example of these men and women of Yah and obey Him wholeheartedly. Let us hold fast to the law of Yah and not get caught up in man-made laws and traditions, whether Jewish or Christian.

Let us *not follow* the man-made tradition of replacing the Mighty One's name with a title.

Let us *not follow* the man-made tradition of disobeying the 4th commandment, the dietary laws given in Lev 11, the observances of the feast days given in Lev 23, and the law concerning physical circumcision given in Gen 17/Lev 12.

Let us start keeping Torah!

"Spirit of the Law"

The Torah can be broken down into two separate components:

1) The inner, the invisible, the spirit, the intent
2) The outer, the visible, the letter, what is written

All Torah is summed up in the commandments found in Due 6:5 and Lev 19:18:

- Love Yah

- Love people

That is to say; all of the commandments of Torah aim to meet one of these two objectives (Mat 22:37-40). This is the *spiritual* component of the Torah alluded to by the apostle Paul in Rom 2:29, 7:6 & 2 Cor 3:6.

This can be applied to any given commandment contained in the Torah.

Take, for instance, the commandments of the Sabbath. (Exo 16, 20, 35, Lev 23, Due 5, Neh 10, Jer 17, Isa 58)

What is written?

1) Do not cook food on the Sabbath (Exo 16:23, 35:3)*

2) Do not work or let anyone within the gates of our community work on the Sabbath (Exo 20:10)*

3) Remember that we were slaves in Egypt and Yah brought us out mightily (Due 5:15)

4) Assemble together onto Yah on the Sabbath (Lev 23:2-3)

5) Do not make purchases on the Sabbath (Neh 10:31) *

6) Do not carry burdens on the Sabbath (Jer 17:7) *

7) Do not pursue secular interests on the Sabbath (Isa 58:13)

*The notable caveat to these prohibitions is when there is an emergency situation (Mat 12:11-12).

Note: These seven *Biblical* laws of the Sabbath were later expanded to 1,521 (39x39) *man-made* laws (Yer. Shab. vii. 2), making the Sabbath impossible to observe.

What is intended?

1) Love Yah by respecting His instruction concerning cooking on the Sabbath

2) Love Yah by respecting His instruction concerning working on the Sabbath

3) Love Yah by never forgetting where we came from and what He did for us

4) Love Yah by respecting His instruction concerning assembling on the Sabbath

5) Love Yah by respecting His instruction concerning conducting business on the Sabbath

6) Love Yah by respecting His instruction concerning heavy lifting on the Sabbath

7) Love Yah by respecting His instruction concerning pursuing secular interests on the Sabbath

These two components of Torah work together in harmony. The spiritual and the literal must both be observed. If one keeps the one, but overlooks the other, the Torah is not being preserved entirely.

If the spirit is broken while the letter is kept, the commandment is being broken.

If one abstains from working on the Sabbath but does not

do it out of love for Yah, the spirit is being broken.

This was the error of most of the Pharisees and still is the error of many religious Jews (Rom 2:27, Mat 15:6, Joh 7:19, Act 7:53, Rom 2:23, Gal 6:13).

If the letter is broken while the spirit is kept, the commandment is being broken.

If one loves Yah but makes purchases on the Sabbath, the letter is being broken.

This was and still is the error of most Christians and Messianic believers.

This truth can be applied to any commandment found in Torah. **Not just ten.** If we are not obeying what is written or if our motive is not to love Yah or love each other, we are missing the mark and are in disobedience to our Heavenly Father.

Let me be clear. We do not obey in order to "get into heaven."

We obey because we love the Heavenly Father and want to please Him.

Joh 14:15

If ye <u>love me</u>, keep my commandments.

Joh 14:21

> He that has my commandments, and keeps them, he it is that <u>loves me</u>

Joh 15:10

> If ye keep my commandments, ye shall <u>abide in my love</u>; even as I have kept my Father's commandments, and abide in his love.

Psa 40:8

> <u>I delight to do your will</u>, O my Mighty One: yea, your <u>law is within my heart</u>.

Rom 7:22

> For <u>I delight in the law</u> of the Mighty One after my inward man.

We obey because we are in a relationship with Him.

1Jn 2:3

> And hereby we do know that <u>we know him</u>, if we keep his commandments.

1Jn 2:4

> He that says, I <u>know him</u>, and keeps not his commandments, is a liar, and the truth is not in him.

** (laws relating to holiness, p.149) There is much confusion about the laws concerning cleanliness. Being unclean due to ejaculation outside of intercourse, touching the carcass of an unclean animal, or touching something a woman on her menstrual cycle has touched is <u>not a prohibition</u>. It just means the person doing so is considered unclean and cannot approach a set-apart sanctuary **until sunset**. This would only be a problem if touching something unclean happens to take place on a weekly Shabbat or annual rest-day.

A husband and wife <u>must</u> not have intercourse during her menstrual cycle (Lev 20:18).

They <u>should</u> also refrain from physical contact altogether on the weekly Sabbath and on the annual rest days during her cycle as his uncleanness would <u>certainly disallow</u> him from entering the sanctuary on the Sabbath. For this reason, they <u>should</u> sleep on a separate bed the night leading into the Sabbath or rest day and not touch the same things the day of (Lev 15:20-23).

For the same reason, she <u>must</u> not enter the sanctuary during her menstrual cycle; or for 40 days after she has given birth to a son and 80 days after she has given birth to a daughter (Lev 15:19; 12:4-5).

Likewise, no one <u>should</u> touch a dead person if they want to enter the sanctuary within seven days (Num 19:11).

These laws are **easier** to follow than choosing to <u>consistently</u> repay evil with good (1 Pe 3:9, Rom 12:17-19, 1 Th 5:15).

Chapter 16
A Sharing Assembly

As the people of Yah, many would agree that our number one priority in life should be to please Him. This is another way of saying we should love Him "with all of our heart/mind, soul and strength" (Deu 6:5/Mar 12:30). However, beyond this, what is our duty as His people?

"That's easy" one might say, "love your neighbor as yourself." (Lev 19:18/Mar 12:31)

While easily said, this single commandment is not so easily expressed.

Two good Biblical examples of this are given in Mathew 19 and Luke 10. Although they happened nearly two thousand years ago, they both apply in the modern day.

Mat 19:16-21

> And, behold, one came and said unto him, Good Master, what good thing shall I do, that I may have eternal life?
>
> And he said unto him, *"Why do you call me good? There is none good but one, that is, the Mighty One: but if you wilt enter into life, keep the commandments."*
>
> He says unto him, Which?
> Yeshua said, *"You shall not murder, You shall not commit adultery, You shall not steal, You*

*shall not bear false witness, Honor your father and your mother: and, You shall **love your neighbor as yourself.***"

The young man says unto him, All these things have I kept from my youth up: what lack I yet?

Yeshua said unto him, *"If you want to be complete, go and **sell that you have, and give to the poor**, and you shall have treasure in heaven: and come and follow me."*

Luk 10:25-37

And, behold, a certain lawyer stood up, and tempted him, saying, Master, what shall I do to inherit eternal life?

He said unto him, *"What is written in the law? how do you read it?"* And he answering said, You shall love Yah your Mighty One with all your heart, and with all your soul, and with all your strength, and with all your mind; and your **neighbor as yourself**.

And he said unto him, *"You have answered right: this do, and you shall live."*

But he, willing to justify himself, said unto Yeshua, And **who is my neighbor**?

And Yeshua answering said, *"A certain man went down from Jerusalem to Jericho, and fell among thieves, which stripped him of his raiment, and wounded him, and departed, leaving him half dead.*

And by chance there came down a certain priest that way: and when he saw him, he passed by on the other side. And likewise a Levite, when he was at the place, came and looked on him, and passed by on the other side.

But a certain Samaritan, as he journeyed, came where he was: and when he saw him, he had compassion on him,

And went to him, and bound up his wounds, pouring in oil and wine, and set him on his own beast, and brought him to an inn, and took care of him. And on the morrow when he departed, he took out two pence, and gave them to the host, and said unto him, Take care of him; and whatsoever you spends more, when I come again, I will repay you.

***Which** now of these three, do you think, **was neighbor unto him** that fell among the thieve?"*

And he said, "He that showed mercy on him."

Then said Yeshua unto him, ***"Go, and do you likewise."***

So how do these two accounts relate?

First, someone comes to Yeshua and asks Him what to do to be saved (Mat 19:16, Luk 10:25).

Then, in response, Yeshua tells him to keep the commandments (Mat 19:17, Luk 10:26-28)—which includes loving your neighbor (Mat 19:19b, Luk 10:27b).

Next, the individual claims to keep them (Mat 19:20, Luk 10:29).

Finally, Yeshua challenges this claim by telling him to do something to demonstrate he truly loves his neighbor (Mat 19:21, Luk 10:36-37).

Our "neighbor" is anyone we show compassion to by offering assistance: whether it be by providing for their needs from our abundance, or by literally saving their lives by tending to their physical wounds.

Thus, while it is easy to say "I love my neighbor," we must actually do so by practically helping them.

The apostles Jacob and John both speak of this practical love in such a way, so as to suggest that to neglect to do it undermines the faith and love we claim to have.

Jas 2:15-17

> **If a brother or sister be naked, and destitute of daily food,** And one of you say unto them, Depart in peace, be *ye* warmed and filled; notwithstanding **ye give them not those things which are needful to the body;** what *doth it* profit? Even so **faith,** if it has not works, **is dead,** being alone."

1Jn 3:17-18

> "But whoso has this world's good, and **sees his brother have need**, and shuts up his bowels *of compassion* from him**, how dwells the love of the Mighty One in him**? My little children, let us not love in word, neither in tongue; but in deed and in truth."

This is our responsibly as believers. This is a major way we love our neighbors as ourselves. In addition to taking care of the brethren, Yeshua also commands us to serve those unbelievers around us who are in need.

Luk 14:12

> Then said he also to him that bade him, "When you make a dinner or a supper, **call not your friends, nor your brethren, neither your kinsmen**, nor your rich neighbors; lest they also bid you again, and a recompense be made you. But when you make a feast, **call the poor, the maimed, the lame, the blind**"

We must conscientiously make an effort to do this as it runs contrary to the ways of the world—our present environment. This is particularly true in the modern age where individualism, coupled with the "American dream," has presented us with the idea that achieving personal wealth is a good thing.

Some have even gone so far as to say that **greed** itself is a good thing because it drives innovation and advances in technology, medicine and societal prosperity. In the words of famed economist Milton Friedman, "the world runs on individuals pursuing their self interests." While this may be true from a secular perspective, we are not of this secular world (see pages 1-4).

As can be seen in the following set of Scriptures, greed is in no way a good thing. Self interests are not something we should be perusing, and personal wealth is not something we should desire.

Mat 6:19-24

> *"Lay not up for yourselves treasures upon earth, where moth and rust doth corrupt, and where thieves break through and steal: But lay up for yourselves treasures in heaven, where neither moth nor rust doth corrupt, and where thieves do not break through nor steal: For **where your treasure is, there will your heart be also**. The light of the body is the eye: **if therefore [you be generous], your whole body shall be full of light**. But if [you be stingy], your whole body shall be full of darkness. If therefore the light that is in you be darkness, how great is that darkness! No man can serve two masters: for either he will hate the one, and love the other; or else he will hold to the one, and despise the other. **Ye cannot serve the Mighty One and money.**"*

Luk 12:13-21

> And one of the company said unto him, "Master, speak to my brother, that he divide the inheritance with me."

> And [Yeshua] said unto him, *"Man, who made me a judge or a divider over you? And he said unto them, Take heed, and* **beware of greed***: for a man's life consists* **not in the abundance of the things which he possesses.**

> *And he spoke a parable unto them, saying, "The ground of a certain rich man produced plentifully: And he thought within himself, saying, 'What shall I do, because I have no room to put my fruits?' And he said, 'This will I do: I will pull down my barns, and build greater; and there will I bestow all my fruits and my goods. And I will say to my soul, Soul, you have much goods laid up for many years; take your ease, eat, drink, and be merry.' But the Mighty One said unto him, 'You fool, this night your soul shall be required of you: then whose shall those things be, which you have provided?'*

> ***So is he that lays up treasure for himself"***

1Ti 6:5-10

> "**Perverse** disputing of **men of corrupt minds**, and destitute of the truth, **supposing that building wealth is devoutness**:

>   from such withdraw yourself.

But devoutness with **contentment** is great gain. For
we brought nothing into *this* world, *and it is* certain
we can carry nothing out. And having food and
clothing **let us be** therewith **content.** But **they that
[desire to] be rich fall into temptation** and a snare,
and *into* many foolish and hurtful lusts, which
drown men in destruction and perdition. For **the
love of money is the root of all evil**: which while
some coveted after, they have erred from the faith"

Jas 5:1-5

"Go to now, *ye* **rich men**, weep and howl for your
miseries that shall come upon *you.* Your riches are
corrupted, and your garments are moth-eaten. Your
gold and silver is cankered; and the rust of them
shall be a witness against you, and shall eat your
flesh as it were fire. **Ye have heaped treasure
together** for the last days. Behold, the hire of the
laborers who have reaped down your fields, which
is of you kept back by fraud, cries: and the cries of
them which have reaped are entered into the ears of
Yah of hosts. **Ye have lived in pleasure on the
earth**, and been greedy"

1 Co 6:10

"Nor thieves, **nor greedy men**, nor drunkards…
shall inherit the kingdom of the Mighty One."

Eph 5:5

"For this ye know, that **no…greedy man…has any
inheritance in the kingdom** of the Messiah"

Col 3:5

> "**Mortify,** therefore your members which are upon the earth; fornication, uncleanness…and **greed**"

Eph 5:3

> "But…all uncleanness, or **greed, let it not be once named among you,** as becomes set-apart ones"

1Pe 2:11

> "Dearly beloved, I beseech *you* as strangers and pilgrims, **abstain from fleshly lusts**, which war against the soul"

Rom 15:1

> "We then that are strong ought to bear the infirmities of the weak, **and not to please ourselves.**"

In Luke 12:33-34, Yeshua tells His disciples:

> *"**Sell your possessions**, and **give generously**; provide yourselves bags which wax not old, a **treasure in the heavens** that fails not, where no thief approaches, neither moth corrupts"*

We can see in the beginning of the book of Acts that His initial disciples took His words literally and did just this.

Act 2:42, 45

> And **they** continued steadfastly in the apostles'
> teaching and fellowship…And **sold their**
> **possessions and goods**, and <u>parted them to all</u> *men,*
> **as every man had need**.

Act 4:34-35

> Neither was there any among them that lacked: for
> **as many as [had] possessors of lands or houses**
> **sold them**, and brought the prices of the things that
> were sold, And laid *them* down at the apostles' feet:
> and **distribution was made unto every man**
> **according as he had need**.

We know from the testimony of Justin Martyr that this
practice continued onto his day (The First Apology, Ch 14).

Sometime **after** the second century, this practice of sharing
possessions with the entire local assembly was abandoned.

Nevertheless, this practice should be restored if we want to
obey Yeshua's words in Luke 12 and follow the example
the first and second generation of Yeshua's disciples left.

In addition to sharing possessions with the *local* assembly,
there is also Biblical precedence for sharing with other
assemblies in need.

Acts 11:27-30 records that there was a famine in the land of
Judea. For this reason, the Assembly of Jerusalem was in
need. Sustenance was provided by the assemblies of

Antioch, Macedonia, Achaia, and Corinth.

Acts 11:29

> "Then the disciples [of Antioch], every man according to his ability, **determined to send relief unto the brethren which dwelt in Judaea:**"

Rom 15:26

> "For it has pleased them of Macedonia and Achaia to make a certain contribution **for the poor set-apart ones which are at Jerusalem**."

2 Co 9:1-2, 7, 12

> "For as touching the **ministering to the set-apart ones**...for which I boast of you to them of **Macedonia, that Achaia** was ready **a year ago**
>
> Every man according as he purposes in his heart, so _let him give_; not grudgingly, or because he has to: for the Mighty One loves a **cheerful giver**.
>
> For the administration of this service not only **supplies the [needs] of the set-apart ones**, <u>but is abundant also by many thanksgivings unto the Mighty One</u>;"

This brings us to a very crucial point. As the underlined selection of the last verse demonstrates, **by supplying the**

needs of other believers we are showing our thanksgiving to Yah.

This practice is both loving our neighbor, and giving thanks to Him.

This being said, we should use the following five guidelines in our sharing:

1) Not give grudgingly, but voluntarily
2) Not give more than we are reasonably able to give
3) Not encourage idleness on the part of the beneficiary
4) Only supply actual needs, and expect the same
5) Supply the needs of fellow believers, but also be generous to everyone

2Co 8:12-15

- For if there be **first a willing mind,**

- *it is* accepted **according to that a man hath,** *and* not according to that he has not.

- For *I mean* **not that other men be eased, and ye burdened:**

- But by an equality, *that* now **at this time your abundance *may be a supply* for their**

[need], that their abundance also may be
***a supply* for your [need]**: that there may be
equality: As it is written,

> "He that *had gathered* much **had
> <u>nothing over</u>; and he that *had
> gathered* little had <u>no lack</u>.**"

3Jn 1:5

- Beloved, you doest faithfully whatsoever
  you <u>doest to the brethren</u> **and** <u>to strangers;</u>

V. Resurrection from the Dead

Chapter 17

Two Resurrections

From the 20th chapter of the book of Revelation, we are clearly taught there will be two different resurrections.

1st Resurrection

Rev 20:4-6

> "And I saw thrones, and they sat upon them, and judgment was given unto them: and *I saw* **the souls** of them that were beheaded for the witness of Yeshua, and for the word of the Mighty One, and which had not worshipped the beast, neither his image, neither had received *his* mark upon their foreheads, or in their hands; and they **lived** and reigned with the Messiah a thousand years.

> But the rest of the dead lived not again until the thousand years were finished. **This** *is* **the first resurrection**.

> Blessed and holy *is* he that has part **in the first resurrection**: on such the second death has no power, but they shall be priests of the Mighty One and of the Messiah, and shall reign with him a thousand years."

2nd Resurrection

Rev 20:11-15

> "And I saw <u>a great white throne</u>, and him that sat on it, from whose face the earth and the heaven fled away; and there was found no place for them. And I saw **the dead**, small and great, **stand before the Mighty One**; and <u>the books were opened</u>: and another book was opened, which is *the book* of life: and the <u>dead were judged</u> out of those things which were written in the books, <u>according to their works</u>. And the sea gave up the dead which were in it; and death and hell delivered up the dead which were in them: and **they were judged every man according to their works**. And death and hates were cast into the lake of fire. This is the second death. And **whosoever was not found written in the book of life was cast into the lake of fire**."

The fact that the resurrection of Rev 20:11-15 happens 1000 years after the resurrection of Rev 20:4-6 is specified in verse 5.

Furthermore, in verse 4 we are told that those who participate in the first resurrection are those who are beheaded for the witness of Yeshua and for the word of the Mighty One; that is, they did not worship the beast or take his image. This is a reference to Rev 13:15.

So now that we know the difference between the two resurrections and who will take part in the first, the question remains, who is left to take part in the second?

There are only three possibilities:

1) Those who are not beheaded because they worship the beast

2) Those who were already died before the beast comes

3) Both

While some may argue that there could be another group of people who neither worship the beast nor get beheaded, Rev 13:5 and 20:4 do not allow this.

Looking at the surrounding verses of each passage and comparing them we can determine that the 1st possibility is at least partially correct.

Rev 13:8

> "And **all that dwell upon the earth** shall worship [the beast], **whose names are not written in the book of Life**"

Rev 20:15

> "And if **anyone** was **not found written in the book of life**, he was thrown into the lake of fire."

Those who worship the beast are not in the book of life and must, therefore, take part in the judgment immediately following the 2nd resurrection of Rev 20:13. It is reasonable to conclude, then, that they take part in this resurrection.

So now that we know that the 1st possibility is at least partially correct, what about the 2nd? Where do the souls of those of those who die before the beast's arrival go?

The following set of Scripture reveals that in the 2nd resurrection, both the righteous and the wicked will participate.

Dan 12:2

> "And many of **them that sleep in the dust of the earth shall awake**, <u>some to everlasting life</u>, and <u>some to shame and everlasting contempt</u>."

Mat 25:46

> "**And these shall go** away <u>into everlasting punishment</u>: **but the righteous** <u>into life eternal</u>."

Joh 5:25, 29

> "Verily, verily, I say unto you, The hour is coming, and now is, <u>when the dead…shall live</u>.
>
> And shall come forth; **they that have done good,** <u>unto the resurrection of life</u>; and **they that have done evil,** <u>unto the resurrection of damnation</u>."

Act 24:15

> "…that there shall be <u>a resurrection of the dead,</u> **both of the just and unjust.**"

Although the 1st possibility is partially correct, this possibility by itself, only allows wicked people destined for the lake of fire to be included in the 2nd resurrection.

Therefore, the 2nd possibility must also be correct.

This ultimately brings us to the 3rd possibility: that both those who worship the beast and take his image *and* those who have died before the beast comes take part in the 2nd resurrection.

The only people that are not included in either resurrection are the 144,000 of Rev 7:3-8, 9:4, & 14:3-5. This is the group that Paul was speaking of in 1 Co 15:51-52, 1 Th 4:15-17 and briefly in 2 Th 2:1. This is explained in greater detail in the next chapter.

Speaking of the 1st resurrection, we are taught:

1Co 15:42-45, 49

> "So also *is* **the [first] resurrection of the dead.** It is sown in corruption; it is raised in incorruption: It is sown in dishonor; <u>it is raised in glory</u>: it is sown in weakness; it is raised in power: It is sown a natural body; <u>it is raised a spiritual body</u>. There is a natural body and there is a spiritual body. And we

have borne the image of the earthy, <u>we shall also
bear the image of the heavenly</u>."

Luk 20:34-36

And Yeshua answering said unto them, "The
children of this world marry, and are given in
marriage: But <u>they which shall be accounted worthy</u>
to obtain that world, and **the [first] resurrection
from the dead,** <u>neither marry,</u> <u>nor are given in
marriage</u>:

<u>Neither can they die any more</u>: for they are equal
unto the angels; and are the children of the Mighty
One <u>being the children of the resurrection</u>."

Eze 37:9-14

"Then said he unto me, 'Prophesy unto the wind,
prophesy, son of man, and say to the wind, Thus
says the Master Yah; Come from the four winds, O
breath, and breathe upon **these slain,** that **they may
live**.' So I prophesied as he commanded me, and the
breath came into them, and they lived, and stood up
upon their feet, <u>an exceeding great army</u>. Then he
said unto me, Son of man, these bones are <u>the whole
house of Israel</u>

Behold, O my people, I will open your graves, and
cause you to **come up out of your graves,** and
bring you into the land of Israel. And ye shall know
that I *am* Yah, when I have opened your graves, O
my people, and brought you up out of your

graves, And <u>shall put my spirit in you</u>, and **ye shall live**, and <u>I shall place you in your own land</u>: then shall ye know that I Yah have spoken *it,* and performed *it,* says Yah.'"

Dan 7:27

"And the <u>kingdom and dominion,</u> and the greatness of the kingdom under the whole heaven, <u>shall be given to the people</u> of the set-apart ones of <u>the most High</u>, whose kingdom *is* an everlasting kingdom"

Rev 20:6

"Blessed and holy *is* he <u>that has part</u> **in the first resurrection**...<u>they</u>...<u>shall reign with</u> [Yeshua] <u>a thousand years</u>."

Chapter 18

End Times Timeline

To get to the end, we will start at the beginning. We will track the years recorded in Scripture in order to understand how old the earth, and creation itself is.

Unless the text clearly indicates otherwise, all Scripture should be taken literally. For example, in the creation week the repeated phrases "and there was evening and there was morning, the nth day" should be understood as referring to literal days.

Biblical Chronology

*For counting purposes, months were not counted (2Sa 2:11/1Ki2:11, 1Ki 6:37-38).

Adam to Seth	130 years (+ .5)*	Gen 5:3
Seth to Enos	105 years (+1)*	Gen 5:6
Enos to Cainan	90 years (+ 1.5)*	Gen 5:9
Cainan to Mahalaleel	70 years (+2)*	Gen 5:12
Mahalaleel to Jared	65 years (+2.5)*	Gen 5:15
Jared to Enoch	162 years (+3)*	Gen 5:18
Enoch to Methuselah	65 years (+3.5)*	Gen 5:21
Methuselah to Lamech	187 years (+4)*	Gen 5:25
Lamech to Noah	182 years (+4.5)*	Gen 5:28
Noah to Shem	502 years (+5)	Gen 7:6,11:10
Shem to Arphaxad	100 years (+5.5)*	Gen 11:10
Arphaxad to Salah	35 years (+6)*	Gen 11:12
Salah to Eber	30 years (+6.5)*	Gen 11:14
Eber to Peleg	34 years (+7)*	Gen 11:16
Peleg to Reu	30 years (+7.5)*	Gen 11:18

Reu to Serug	32 years (+8)* Gen 11:20
Serug to Nahor	30 years (+8.5)* Gen 11:22
Nahor to Terah	29 years (+9)* Gen 11:24
Terah to Promice	205 years Gen 11:32, 12:4, Act 7:1-5
Promise to Exodus (EX)	430 years Exo 12:40-41**,
	Gen 12:4-5/Gal 3:17
Total	2513 years (≤2523 years*)

EX to Solomon's reign (SR)	415 years (+ .5)* 1Ki 6:1
SR to Rehoboam's reign (AR)	40 years (+1)* 2Ch 9:30
AR to Abijah's reign (ABR)	17 years (+1)* 2Ch 12:13
ABR to Asa's reign	3 years (+2)* 2Ch 13:2
Asa's reign to Jeho's reign	41 years (+2.5) 2Ch 16:13
Jeho's reign to Joram's reign	25 years (+3)* 2Ch 20:31
Joram's reign to Ahaziah's	8 years (+3.5)* 2Ch 21:5
Ahaziah's reign to Athaliah's	1 year (+4)* 2Ch 22:2
Athaliah's reign to Joash's	6 years " 2Ch 22:10-12
Joash's reign to Amaziah's	40 years (+5)* 2Ch 24:1
Amaziah's reign to Uzziah's	29 years (+5.5)* 2Ch25:1
Uzziah's reign to Jotham's	52 years (+6)* 2Ch 26:3
Jotham's reign to Ahaz's	16 years (+6.5)* 2Ch 27:1
Ahaz's reign to Hezekiah's	16 years (+7)* 2Ch 28:1
Hezekiah's reign to Manasseh's	29 years (+7.5) 2Ch 29:1
Manasseh's reign to Amon's	55 years (+8)* 2Ch 33:1
Amon's reign to Josiah's (JOR)	2 years (+8.5) 2Ch33:21
JRO to Jehoahaz's reign (JR)	31 years (+9)* 2Ch 34:1
JR to Jehoiakim's reign (JHK)	0 years (+9.5)* 2Ch36:2
JHK's reign to Jehoiachin's reign	11 years (+10)* 2Ch36:5
Jehoiachin's to Zedekiah's reign	0 years (+10.5) 2Ch36:9
Zedekiah's reign to captivity	11 years (+11) 2Ch 36:11
(629 BCE)	
Captivity to decree	70 years 2Ch 36:20-22

Haggai and Zechariah started prophesying between 629 and 559 BCE (Ezr 5:1-2)
Daniel 9 took place in the year 519 BCE (Dan 9:1, Ezr 1:1, 6:15, Joh 2:20)

Ezra came to Jerusalem out of Babylon in 458 BCE (Ezr 7:8,1)

Total   918 years (≤929 years*)

Grand total: 3431 years (≤3452 years*)

Decree given to rebuild the Temple (first year of Cyrus the great) −559 BCE

+ 558 years (Ezr 6:3)

+2016 years (1 BCE to 2016 CE)

Current year:
(corresponds to 2016-17)   6005 (≤6026*)

Next Jubilee year begins
(corresponds to 2044***)   6033 (≤6054)

**Samaritan Pentateuch & Septuagint

This also aligns with other Scriptures (Gen 46:11, Exo 6:18, 6:20), where the traditional view supported by the middle ages manuscript of Exo 12:40-41 does not.

Exo 7:7 states that Moses was 80 years old when he led the children of Israel out of Egypt.

The Masoretic of Exo 12:40-41 says that the children of Israel were in Egypt for 430 years.

Therefore, according to the Masoretic text, Moses was born 350 years into the ancient Israelites sojourning in Egypt (430-80).

Gen 46:11 states Kohath, son of Levi, was with the company of Israel that entered Egypt.

Exo 6:18 states that Kohath, son of Levi, was the father of Amram.

Exo 6:20 says that Amram, son of Kohath, was the father of Moses.

Therefore, according to the Masoretic text, from Kohath to Moses (2 generations) was 350 years. This would mean that Korath had Amram when he was approximately **175** years old and Amram had Moses when he was approximately **175** years old. **This would contradict Exo 6:18 & 6:20.**

On the other hand:

Scripture records that Abraham was given the promise when he was 75 years old (Gen 12:1-4).

Scripture records that when Abraham gave birth to Isaac, he was 100 years old (Gen 21:5).

Therefore, from the promise given to Abraham to the birth of Isaac 25 years had elapsed (100-25).

Scripture records that when Isaac gave birth to Jacob when he was 60 years old (Gen 25:26).

Scripture records that when Jacob entered Egypt, he was 130 years old (Gen 47:9).

Therefore, from the promise given to Abraham to the beginning of the sojourning in Egypt, 215 years had elapsed (25+60+130).

Scripture reveals that the Torah was given through Moses in the same year of the exodus (Exo 19:1).

Scripture reveals that from the time Abraham received the promise to the time the Torah was given was 430 years (Gal 3:17).

Therefore, the time the children of Israel sojourned in Egypt was 215 years (430-215).

Exo 7:7 states that Moses was 80 years old when he led the children of Israel out of Egypt.

Therefore, according to Gal 3:17, Moses was born 135 years into the ancient Israelites sojourning in Egypt (215-80).

This would mean that Korath and Amram each had their child at the approximate age of **67.5. This does not contradict Exo 6:18 & 6:20.**

***The theory that the next Jubilee falls in the year 2044 is based on four things.

1) The Jubilee is counted every 49 years

> Lev 25:8 tells us to count 49 years. Then the next two verses tell us to proclaim the year of Jubilee with a rams horn on the tenth day of the seventh month. There is no room in this passage for an addition of nearly six months.

> In Lev 25:11 we are told that no planting is to be done in the year of Jubilee. Then, ten verses later,

we are told to plant in the year immediately following the seventh year. It was already established that the 49th year was also the seventh year (verse 8). Thus, we can see that the 50th year would be the eighth year, the year immediately following the seventh year. If the 50th year began and ended at the same time the eighth year did, then there would be a contradiction in the passage.

Thus, we can see that the 50th year, the year of Jubilee, begins in the 49th year and ends half way into the 50th year, allowing planting to be done in the latter half of the eighth year.

2) The first Jubilee must have been celebrated between the years 1380 and 1391 BCE.

49 + 7 years after the children of Israel first entered the Promised Land. [558+(918 to 929) -40 -49 -7].

3) The Jubilee cycle also follows the Sabbath year cycle, as the 49th year is also the 7th year.

4) The Sabbath year cycle has been established by the research carried out by Qadesh La Yahweh Press.

Now that we have a solid understanding of the past, let us look to the future.

According to the Merriam-Webster dictionary, the word eschatology is *a branch of theology concerned with the final events in the history of the world or of humankind.*

A PROPOSED ESCHATOLOGICAL CHRONOLOGY

03/22/60__   -A week long covenant is confirmed by a
(5/10/2037)   coming anointed prince. Dan 9:27

03/25/60__   -The continual offerings are taken away.
        Dan 9:27, 11:31

+1290 days   -Dan 12:11

10/25/60__   -Abomination of desolation set up in the
        third Temple. Dan 11:31, Mat 24:15

+1010 days   -Dan 8:14. (2300 - 1290)

8/15/60__   -The holy place will be made right.
        Dan 8:14

+325 days   -(1335-1010). Dan 12:12

7/10/60__   -144,000 delivered out of Jerusalem before
        its destruction. Joe 2:32, Isa 4:2-3, 6:13,
        10:20, 37:32, Oba 1:17, Zec 14:2, Luk 21:24,
        Rev 7:2-8,   9:3-4, 12:6, 12, 17, 14:1, 12

+1260 days   -Jerusalem is plundered. Dan 7:25, 8:11-12. 9
        26-27, 11:31-36, 12:7, Zec 14:2, Luk 21:24,
        Rev 11:2, 5, 7

+ 3.5 days   -The two witnesses are killed and come back
        to life. Rev 11:7-11

1/14/60__   -The day of wrath and the return of Yeshua
        occurs. Isa 27:13, Isa 30:30, 31:5, Dan
        7:13-14, 27, Joe 2:1/23, Mic 5:2/4/6/15,
        Zep 1:18, 3:8, Zec 12:10, Mal 4:1-2, Mat
        24:31, 1Co 15:52, 1Th 4:16, Rev 11:15.

+1000 years   -The beheaded reign with Yeshua. Dan 7:12-
                 14, 26-27, 8:25, 1Chr 17:12, Zec 6:13, Rev
                 20:2-6, 1Eno 90:29-30, 91:14-15

1/15/70__   -Battle of Gog and Magog takes place. Rev
                 20:7- 9

1/15/70__   -The final judgment occurs. Mat 25:31-32,
                 Rev 20:11-15

1/15/70__   -New heavens and earth are created;
                 Jerusalem descends from the heavens and
                 the righteous live forever, with no end. Rev
                 21:1-22:15

The remainder of this chapter will focus on the 1263.5 days that is commonly referred to as the "great tribulation" (the sectioned off in the above chronology). The following section will deal with what will specifically happen during this time. The next and final section will provide an overview of this time period to show the significance of the Day of Atonement and Passover in the end times.

The Great Tribulation

Paul teaches that before Yeshua returns, the false Messiah will come.

2 Th 2:1-3

> "Now we beseech you, brethren, by the coming of our Master Yeshua...**that day shall not come**, except there come a falling away **first**, and that **man of sin be revealed**"

The following phrase represents a bit of a mystery:

"time and times and half a time"

What is the meaning?

A common understanding is that *a time* refers to a year, *times* refers to two years, and *half and time* refers to half a year. Thus, *"a time and times and half a time"* signifies three and a half years.

Can this understanding be supported with Scripture?

Dan 7:25

> "…and it speaks words against the Most High, and it <u>wears out the set-apart ones</u> of the Most High, and it intends to change appointed times and law, and <u>they are given into its hand</u> for **a time and times and half a time**."

This verse is actually a reiteration of a previous verse:

Dan 7:21

> "I was looking, and **this horn** was <u>fighting against the set-apart ones, and was prevailing against them</u>"

Here it is saying that the set-apart ones of the Most High are given into the hand of this "horn" for "a time and times and half a time."

Who is this *horn*?

Dan 8:9-11

> And from one of them came **a little horn** which
> became exceedingly great toward the south, and
> toward the east, and toward the Splendid *Land*. And
> it became great, up to the host of the heavens. And
> it caused some of the host and some of the stars to
> fall to the earth, and trampled them down. It even
> exalted itself as high as the Prince of the host. And
> **it took that which is continual** away from Him,
> and threw down the foundation of His set-apart
> place.

Here it is said that this same "horn" is the one who will
take away that which is continual. This passage is thus
linked to Dan 9:27, which says:

> "And he shall confirm a covenant with many for
> one week. And in the middle of the week **he shall
> put an end to slaughtering and meal offering.
> And on the wing of abominations he shall lay
> waste**"

And also to Dan 11:31, which says:

> "And strong ones shall arise from him and profane
> the set-apart place, the stronghold, and shall **take
> away that which is continual, and set up the
> abomination that lays waste**"

The fact that Dan 11:31 is making reference to the same
individual in Dan 7:25, is further verified in the comparison
of Dan 11:36 with Dan 7:8 & 7:25:

Dan 11:36

> "And the sovereign shall...**speak incredible matters against the Mighty One** of Mighty Ones, and shall prosper until the wrath has been accomplished – for what has been decreed shall be done"

Dan 7:8

> "...then saw another horn, a little one, coming up among them...And see...and a **mouth speaking great** *words*."

Dan 7:25

> "and **it speaks words against the Most High**"

By now, it should be obvious that this individual is the same individual spoken of in Rev 13:5-7:

> "And he was given a mouth **speaking great** *matters* and blasphemies, and <u>he was given authority to do so forty-two months</u>. And **he opened his mouth in blasphemies against the Mighty One**, to blaspheme His Name, and His Tent, and those dwelling in the heaven. And <u>it was given to him to fight with the set-apart ones and to overcome them</u>. And authority was given to him over every tribe and tongue and nation."

Now that we can see that the individual spoken of in Rev 13 is the same individual spoken of in 2Th 2, Dan 11, Dan 9, Dan 8 & Dan 7, let us look again at the opening passage:

Dan 7:25

> "and it speaks words against the Most High, and it
> wears out the set-apart ones of the Most High, and it
> intends to change appointed times and law, and they
> are given into its hand for a time and times and half
> a time."

Comparing these passages, we can see that this individual
is given authority over the set-apart ones for "a time and
times and half a time" or 42 months.

$$42 \text{ months} = 12 \times 3.5$$

In other words, the phrase *"a time and times and half a
time"* is, in fact, three and a half years.

Now that is understanding is validated, let us move on to
another place this phrase is used.

Rev 12:14

> "And the woman was given two wings of a great
> eagle, to fly into the wilderness to her place, where
> she is nourished for **a time and times and half a
> time**, from the presence of the serpent."

Who is the woman?

Rev 12:1-5

> "And a great sign was seen in the heaven: a woman
> clad with the sun, with the moon under her feet, and

on her head a crown of twelve stars. And <u>being</u> <u>pregnant</u>, she cried out in labor and in <u>pain</u> to give birth. And <u>she bore a male child who was to</u> <u>shepherd all nations with a rod of iron. And her</u> <u>child was caught away to the Mighty One</u> and to His throne."

Here is seems obvious that this woman is the mother of Yeshua.

Furthermore, this passage bears striking resemblance to a prophecy in Isaiah 66:7-8

"Before <u>she labored, she gave birth</u>; before a <u>pain</u> came to her, she was delivered of <u>a male child</u>. Who has heard the like of this? Who has seen the like of these? Is a land brought forth in one day? Is a nation born at once? For as soon as Zion labored, she gave birth to her children."

Here it seems obvious that this woman, the mother of Yeshua, is Zion.

So now that the identity of the woman is partially known, who is she escaping from?

Rev 12:14

"And <u>the woman was given two wings of a great</u> <u>eagle, to fly into the wilderness to her place</u>, where she is nourished for a time and times and half a time, <u>from the presence of the serpent</u>."

Why is she escaping from the serpent?

Rev 12:13

> "And when the dragon saw that he had been thrown
> to the earth, he persecuted the woman who gave
> birth to the male child."

It seems she is escaping the serpent's persecution.

What does the serpent do next?

Rev 12:15-17

> "And *out of his mouth the serpent spewed* water like
> a river after the woman, to cause her to be swept
> away by the river. And the earth helped the woman,
> and the earth opened its mouth and swallowed up
> the river *which the dragon had spewed out of his
> mouth*. And the dragon was enraged with the
> woman, and he went to fight with **the remnant** of
> her seed, those **guarding the commands** of the
> Mighty One and **possessing the witness** of Yeshua
> the Messiah."

He goes to fight the remnant. Who is the remnant?

Rev 6:9

> "And when He opened the fifth seal, I saw under
> the altar the beings of those having been slain for
> **the Word** of the Mighty One and for **the witness**
> which they held, and they cried with a loud voice,
> saying, "How long, O Master, set-apart and true,
> until You judge and avenge our blood on those who
> dwell on the earth?" And there was given to each

one a white robe, and they were told that they
should rest a little while longer, until both *the
number of* their fellow servants and their brothers,
who would be killed as they were, was completed."

Rev 7:13 -14

"And one of the elders responded, saying to me,
'Who are these dressed in white robes, and where
did they come from?' And I said to him, 'Master,
you know.' And he said to me, 'These are those
coming out of the great distress, having washed
their robes and made them white in the blood of the
Lamb.'"

Rev 20:4

"And I saw thrones – and they sat on them, and
judgment was given to them – and the lives of those
who had been beheaded because of **the witness** they
bore to Yehsua and because of **the Word** of the
Mighty One, and who did not worship the beast, nor
his image, and did not receive his mark upon their
foreheads or upon their hands"

If the remnant are those who come out of the great
tribulation (Rev 7:14) and are beheaded because they did
not worship the beast (Rev 20:4), then they are the ones
who seem to be subject to the authority given to the beast
of Rev 13:7

"And it was given to him to fight with the set-apart
ones and to overcome them. And authority was
given to him over every tribe and tongue and nation."

This takes us back to Rev 12:17:

> "And the dragon was enraged with the woman, and he went <u>to fight with the remnant of her seed</u>, those guarding the commands of the Mighty One and possessing the witness of Yeshua the Messiah."

It would seem, then, that period given in Rev 12:14 is the same period of Rev 13:5: the three and a half years of the beast/man of sin/ king/coming prince/little horn.

Thus, it would appear as though Zion is rescued from this period of time.

Rev 12:14

> "And the woman was given two wings of a great eagle, <u>to fly into the wilderness</u> to her place, <u>where she is nourished</u> for a time and times and half a time, <u>from the presence of the serpent</u>."

Who is Zion?

Rev 9:3-4

> "And out of the smoke locusts came upon the earth, and authority was given to them as the scorpions of the earth possess authority. And it was said to them that they shall not harm the grass of the earth, or any green *matter*, or any tree, but <u>only those men who do not have the seal of the Mighty One upon their foreheads</u>."

Rev 7:2-4

>"And I saw another messenger coming up from the
>rising of the sun, holding the seal of the living
>Mighty One. And he cried with a loud voice to the
>four angels to whom it was given to harm the earth
>and the sea, saying, "<u>Do not harm the earth, nor the
>sea, nor the trees until we have sealed the servants
>of our Mighty One upon their foreheads.</u>
>And I heard the number of those who were sealed,
>**one hundred and forty-four thousand**, sealed out
>of all the tribes of the children of Israel"

Rev 14:3

>"And they sang a renewed song before the throne,
>and before the four living creatures, and the elders.
>And no one was able to learn that song except the
>**hundred and forty-four thousand** <u>who were
>redeemed from the earth</u>."

Thus, it seems clear that "Zion," the 144,000, will not have
to endure the tribulation described in Rev 6-9 and 15-16,
which is also the period of time given in Rev 11, 12 & 13.

It also appears that this time will end when the event
described in Rev 6:12-17, 11:15-19, & 19:11-21 takes
place:

Rev 6:12-17

>"And I looked when He opened the sixth seal and
>saw **a great earthquake came to be**. And **the sun
>became black** as sackcloth of hair, and **the moon
>became as blood**. And the stars of the heaven fell
>to the earth, as a fig tree drops its unripe figs, being

shaken by a strong wind. And **heaven departed like a scroll being rolled up**, and every mountain and island was moved out of its place. And the sovereigns of the earth, and the great ones, and the rich ones, and the commanders, and the mighty, and every slave and every free one, hid themselves in the caves and in the rocks of the mountains, and said to the mountains and rocks, 'Fall on us and hide us from the face of Him sitting on the throne and from the **wrath of the Lamb**, because **the great day of His wrath has come**, and who is able to stand?'"

Rev 11:15, 18-19

"And the seventh messenger sounded, and there came to be loud voices in the heaven, saying, 'The reign of this world has become *the reign* of our Master, and of His Messiah, and He shall reign forever and ever!' And the nations were enraged, and **Your wrath has come**, and the time of the dead to be judged, and to give the reward to Your servants the prophets and to the set-apart ones, and to those who fear Your Name, small and great, and to destroy those who destroy the earth. And the Dwelling Place of the Mighty One was **opened in the heaven**, and the ark of His covenant was seen in His Dwelling Place. And there **came to be** lightning, and voices, and thunders, and **an earthquake**, and great hail."

Rev 19:11, 13, 19-20

"And I saw the heaven opened, and there was **a white horse**. And **He who sat on him** was called Trustworthy and True, and in righteousness **He**

judges and fights…and having been dressed in a robe dipped in blood – and His Name is called: The Word of Yah. And I saw the beast, and the sovereigns of the earth, and their armies, gathered together to **fight Him who sat on the horse** and His army. And **the beast was seized**, and with him the false prophet who worked signs in his presence, by which he led astray those who received the mark of the beast and those who worshipped his image. The two were thrown alive into the lake of fire"

The Day of Yah

Prophecy speaks of a coming day when there will be a sound of a shofar, signaling a gathering of Yah's chosen:

*"And He shall send His angels with a great **sound of a [shofar]**, and **they shall gather together His chosen ones** from the four winds, from one end of the heavens to the other."*

-Mat 24:31

*"And in that day it shall be that a great **[shofar] is blown**, and…you **shall be gathered** one by one, O children of **Israel**."*

-Isa 27:13-14

Scripturally, there is only one day of the year when a shofar is commanded to be sounded:

*"You shall then **sound a [shofar]** to pass through **on the tenth day of the seventh month**, on the Day of Atonement cause a shofar to pass through all your land."*

-Lev 25:9

At the time of His second coming, Yeshua will call out liberty (Isa 61:1).

> *"And you shall set the fiftieth year apart, and **call out liberty** throughout all the land to all its inhabitants, it is a Jubilee for you"*
>
> -Lev 25:10

Likewise, according to Scripture, at this time, Israel will dwell in safety (Jer 23:6, 33:16).

> *"and the land shall yield its fruit, and **you shall** eat to satisfaction, and shall **dwell there in safety.**"*
>
> -Lev 25:19

At this time, we will be returned to our inheritances (Isa 49:8).

> *"In the Year of this Jubilee let each one of you **return to his possession.**"*
>
> -Lev 25:13

Notice that both occasions:

1) begin with the sounding of a shofar (Lev 25:9, Isa 27:13-14, Mat 24:31)

2) call out liberty (Lev 25:10, Isa 61:1)

3) commence safe dwelling (Lev 25:19, Jer 33:6, 33:16)

4) involve returning to our tribe's original inheritances (Lev 25:13, Isa 49:8)

Could it be more than just a coincidence? Could it be that the signal of the last days, relating to Yeshua's return will be none other than the Day of Atonement, when the year of Jubilee is to be proclaimed?

Prophecy reveals that Yeshua will come again to:

> "*Proclaim...the* **day of vengeance**"
>
> -Isa 61:2

Speaking of the time of the His second coming, Yeshua informs us:

> "*Because these are* **days of vengeance**, *to fill all that have been written. And when you see* **Jerusalem surrounded** *by armies, then know that its laying waste is near.* And then they shall see the Son of Adam coming in a cloud"
>
> -Luk 21:22-23, 27

Here we can see that Yeshua's return is connected to Jerusalem being surrounded.

Speaking of the same time-frame, the prophets reveal:

> "*And I shall* **gather all the gentiles** *to* **battle against Jerusalem**. *And the city shall be taken, the houses plundered, and the women ravished. Half of the city shall go into exile, but the remnant of the people shall not be cut off from the city. See, a* **day** *shall come* **of Yah**, *and your spoil shall be divided in your midst.*"
>
> -Zec 14:2, 1.

Here we can see that the time of Yeshua's return is also connected to the day of Yah.

*"For the day is near, even the **day of Yah** is near. It is a day of clouds, the **time of the Gentiles**."*

-Eze 30:3

Here we can see that the day of Yah is also called the time of the Gentiles. Continuing on with His prophecy, Yeshua tells us:

*"And they shall fall by the edge of the sword, and be led away captive into all nations. And **Jerusalem** shall be **trampled** underfoot by the **Gentiles** until the **times of the Gentiles** are filled."*

-Luk 21:24

Speaking of this time, the John prophecies that:

*"But cast out the court which is outside the Dwelling Place, and do not measure it, for it has been given to the **Gentiles**, and they shall **trample** the **set-apart city** under foot for **forty-two months**."*

-Rev 11:2

Here we can see that this "time of the Gentiles" lasts 42 months.

*"And he was given a mouth <u>speaking</u> great matters and <u>blasphemies</u>, and he was given authority to do so **forty-two months**. And it was given to him to <u>fight with the set-apart ones</u> and to <u>overcome</u> them."*

-Rev 13:5, 7

*"it <u>speaks words against</u> the Most High, and...<u>wears out the set-apart ones</u>...and <u>they are given into its hand</u> for a **time and times and half a time**."*

-Dan 7:25

Here we can see that 42 months is also called "a time and times and half a time."

> *"And the <u>woman</u> was given two wings of a great eagle, to fly into <u>the wilderness</u> to her place, where she is <u>nourished</u> for **a time and times and half a time**, from the presence of the serpent."*
>
> *-Rev 12:14*

> *"And the <u>woman</u> fled into <u>the wilderness</u>, where she has a place prepared by the Mighty One, <u>to be nourished</u> there **one thousand two hundred and sixty days**."*
>
> *-Rev 12:6*

We can see here that 42 months, or "a time and times and half a time," is also 1260 days.

John continues this prophecy by stating that immediately following this time:

> *"And after the <u>three and a half days</u> a spirit of life from Mighty One entered into them, and they stood upon their feet, and great fear fell on those who saw them. And the **seventh messenger sounded**, and there came to be loud voices in the heaven, saying, 'The reign of this world has become the reign of our Master, and of His Messiah"*
>
> -Rev 11:3, 7, 11,15

Referring to this final sounding, the apostle Paul tells us:

> *"In a moment, in the twinkling of an eye, at the **last** trumpet. For the **trumpet shall sound**, and the **dead shall be raised"***
>
> -1Co 15:52

*"Because **the Master Himself shall come down from heaven** with a shout, **with the** voice of a chief messenger, and with the **trumpet** of Mighty One, and the **dead** in the Messiah **shall rise** first."*

-1Th 4:16

The prophecy continues with foretelling an event regarding a SECOND gathering of the nations around Jerusalem:

*"And in that day it shall be that I make Jerusalem a very heavy stone for all peoples – all lifting it are severely injured. And all the nations of the earth shall be gathered against it. In that day Yah **shall shield the inhabitants of Jerusalem**."*

-Zec 12:3

Speaking of the same time, Isaiah prophecies:

*"Though Yah gave you bread of adversity and water of affliction, your Teacher shall no longer be hidden. But your eyes shall see your Teacher... See, the Name of Yah is coming from afar, burning with His wrath, and heavy smoke. His lips shall be filled with rage, and His tongue be as a devouring fire; Let the song be to you **as in a night set apart for a festival**... And Yah **shall** cause His excellent voice to be heard, and **show the coming down of His Arm**, with raging wrath and the flame of a consuming fire, with scattering, downpour and hailstones."*

-Isa 30:20, 27, 29, 30

Prophecy reveals that this "Arm" of Yah is Yeshua.

*"Who has believed our report? And to whom was **the Arm** of Yah revealed?"*

-Isa 53:1

Prophecy also reveals that His "Arm" will turn back captivity:

*"The Spirit of the Master Yah is upon Me...He has sent Me to bind up the broken-hearted, to proclaim **release to the captives**"*

-Isa 61:1

Speaking of this time, the Prophets reveal:

*"For look, in those days and at that time, when **I turn back the captivity of Judah and Jerusalem**"*

-Joe 3:1

*"Like hovering birds, so does Yah of hosts **protect Jerusalem** – protecting and delivering, **passing over (Pesach)** and rescuing...For in that day...his commanders shall be afraid of the **Banner**"*

-Isa 31:5, 7, 9

Prophecy reveals that this "Banner" is Yeshua:

*"And in that day there shall be a Root of Jesse, standing as a **Banner**"*

-Isa 11:10

*"Thus said the Master Yah, 'See, I...set up My **Banner** for the peoples'"*

-Isa 49:22

Speaking of this time, Zechariah also reveals:

> *"And I shall pour on the house of David and on the*
> *inhabitants of Jerusalem a spirit of favor and prayers.*
> *And **they shall look on Me whom they pierced**, and*
> *they shall **mourn for Him** as one mourns for his only*
> *son. And they shall be in bitterness over Him as*
> *bitterness over the first-born."*
>
> -Zec 12:10

So at the time of this Passover (Isa 30:29, 31:5), Yah will:

> *"show the coming down of His [Messiah]... And [the*
> *inhabitants of Jerusalem] shall look on [Yeshua] whom*
> *they pierced...and shall morn for Him"*
>
> -Isa 30:30, Zec 12:10

From 7/10 until the going down of the sun on 1/14 three and a half years later, there are 1263.5 counted days using the Biblical calendar.

In conclusion, the day of Yah is a prophetic term referring to 1263.5 days beginning on Yom Kippur, the beginning of the final year of Jubilee, and ending on the on the final Passover day, three and a half years later.

This is again confirmed in the Septuagint version of the Renewed Covenant chapter of the prophet Jeremiah 31:6-9

"For it is a day when [the Nazarenes] that plead on the mountains of Ephraim shall call, saying, Arise

ye, and go up to Zion to Yah your Mighty One. For thus says Yah to Jacob; Rejoice ye, and exult over the head of the nations: make proclamation, and praise ye: say, **Yah has delivered his people, the remnant of Israel.** *Behold, I bring them from the north,* **and will gather them from the end of the earth to the feast of the Passover**...*for I am become a father to Israel and Ephraim is my first-born."*

VI. Eternal Judgment

Chapter 19
Hades and Gehenna

The English word *hell* in the traditional "New Testament" (the Greek version) is a translation from two different words: *hades* (G86) and *gehenna* (G1067).

The word *hades* means *the grave* or *place of the dead*. It corresponds to the Hebrew word *sheol* (H7585).

While the word *gehenna* originally referred to the valley of Hinnom, it is figuratively used to refer to *a place of **eternal punishment***. This Greek word is simply a transliteration of the Hebrew term for *valley of Hinnom* (H1516 and H2011) used three times in the Hebrew Scriptures (Jos 15:8, 18:16 & Neh 11:30) and ten additional places as *valley of the son of Hinnom*.

The real difference between *Hades* and *Gehenna* is that while *Hades* is currently full of people, **Gehenna is a place that does not currently exist**.

Hades/Sheol

Gen 42:38

> And[Jacob] said "…if mischief befall [Joseph] by the way in the which ye go, then shall ye bring down <u>my gray hairs with sorrow **to [Sheol]**</u>."

Num 16:33

> They and all that *appertained* to them <u>went down</u>
> <u>alive into **[Sheol]**</u>, and the earth closed upon them

1Sa 2:6

> "Yah kills, and makes alive: he <u>bring down to</u>
> **[Sheol]**, and bring up."

Psa 89:48

> "<u>What man</u> *is he that* lives, and <u>shall not see</u> death?
> shall he deliver his soul from the hand of **[Sheol]**?"

Eze 31:17

> "<u>They also went down **into [sheol]**</u> with him unto
> *them that be* slain with the sword"

Luk 16:23

> "And **in [Hades]**] he lift up his eyes, being in
> torments, and saw <u>Abraham</u> afar off"

Rev 20:13

> "And…**[Hades]** delivered up <u>the dead which were</u>
> <u>in them</u>"

Notice how all people (Psa 89:48) both wicked and
righteous people such as Abraham (Luk 16:23) and Jacob

(Gen 42:38) are destined for *Hades* when they die. After all, *Hades* simply means *the grave*.

Gehenna

Mat 5:29

> "And if your right eye offend you, pluck it out, and cast *it* from you: for it is profitable for you that one of your members should perish, and not *that* your whole <u>body should be cast **into [Gehenna]**</u>."

Mat 18:8-9

> "Wherefore if your hand or your foot offend you, cut them off, and cast *them* from you: it is better for you to enter into life halt or maimed, rather than having two hands or two feet to be <u>cast into everlasting fire</u>. And if your eye offend you, pluck it out, and cast *it* from you: it is better for you to enter into life with one eye, rather than having two eyes <u>to be cast **into [Gehenna]** fire</u>."

Mar 9:43-44

> "And if your hand offend you, cut it off: it is better for you to enter into life maimed, than having two hands to go **into [Gehenna]**, into <u>the fire that never shall be quenched</u>: Where <u>their worm dies not, and the fire is not quenched</u>."

Luk 12:5

> "But I will forewarn you whom ye shall fear: Fear him, which <u>after he has killed</u> has power to <u>cast **into**</u>

[Gehenna]; yea, I say unto you, Fear him."

Notice how *Gehenna* is equated with "everlasting fire" (Mat 18:8-9) and "the fire that never shall be quenched, where worm dies not" (Mar 9:43-44). This latter phrase is used in the book of Isaiah, which speaks of a time after the creation of the new heavens and earth.

Isa 66:22,24

> "For as the new heavens and the new earth, which I will make, shall remain before me, says Yah, so shall your seed and your name remain.
>
> And they shall go forth, and look upon the carcasses of the men that have transgressed against me: for **their worm shall not die, neither shall their fire be quenched**; and they shall be an abhorring unto all flesh."

The concept of "everlasting fire" is also present in Revelation 20, which also describes an event that takes place after the final judgement, which is after the millennial reign.

Rev 20:11-15, 20

> "And I saw a great white throne…And I saw the dead, small and great, stand before the Mighty One
>
> And the sea gave up the dead which were in it; and death and [Hedes] delivered up the dead which were in them: and they were judged every man according to their works. And death and [hades] were cast into

the **lake of fire**. This is the **second death**.

(This "second death" is what Luk 12:5 was referring to. See p. 221)

And whosoever was not found written in the book of life <u>was cast into the **lake of fire**</u>.

And the devil that deceived them <u>was cast into the **lake of fire**</u>...<u>and shall be tormented day and night for ever and ever</u>."

Chapter 20
Enoch and the End Times

The book of Enoch or *1 Enoch* is comprised of five sections. There is good reason to believe that the whole book, all five sections, should be considered Divinely inspired Scripture. The following documents this reason:

The first section is clearly quoted by the apostle Jude and is called prophecy.

Jud 14-15

> "And Enoch, the seventh from Adam, also prophesied of these, saying: '**See, Yah comes with His myriads of set-apart ones, to execute judgment on all, to punish all** who are wicked among them concerning **all their** wicked **works which they have committed** in a wicked way, **and** concerning **all the harsh words which** wicked **sinners have spoken against Him.**'"

Eno 1:9

> "**See, He comes with myriads of His set-apart ones, to execute judgment on all**, and **to punish all** the ungodly, and to convict all flesh of **all their works** of ungodliness **which they have** ungodly **committed, and** of **all the harsh words which** ungodly **sinners have spoken against Him.**"

In the second section, there are more than 30 references to Yeshua, including many references to Him as the "Son of Man" –a term He uses for Himself multiple times in the "gospels," and used by Steven in the book of Acts, the "Righteous one" –a term used for Him in Acts 7:52 and 22:14, the "Chosen One" –a term used for Him in Isa 42:1 and Luke 23:35, and the "Anointed One" –a term that, when transliterated from the Hebrew, is *haMashiach* or the Messiah.

This section also makes mention of the Renewed Covenant (1Eno 60:6), the seven Sprits of Yah given to Yeshua (1Eno 49:3, 51:3, & 67:10) –also spoken of in Isa 11:2, Rev 1:5, 3:1, 4:5 & 5:6, the Word of Yeshua's mouth slaying the sinners (1Eno 62:2) –also spoken of in Rev 19:15, the new heavens and new earth (1Eno 44:4-5) –also spoken of in Isa 65:17, 66:22 & Rev 21:1-22:15 (particularly 1Eno 44:5c with Rev 22:15), the angels of Yah's wrath (1Eno 53:3, 62:11, & 63:1) – also spoken of in Rev 15:7, eternal light (1Eno 58:5-6) –also spoken of in Isa 60:19 and Rev 22:5, judgment day being prepared for those who disobey (1Eno 60:6) –also spoken of in Isa 24:5 & Mic 5:15, the first resurrection of the dead (62:15) –also spoken of in Rev 20:4-5, and the second resurrection of the dead (1Eno 51:1), also spoken of in Rev 20:13. It also speaks of us being given new garments (1Eno 62:15-16) –details also mentioned in Mat 22:11, Rev 3:5 & 7:9, and all sinners falling on their knees and confessing before Yeshua (1Eno 62:9 & 63:1) –also spoken of in Isa 45:23-24 & Phil 2:10-11.

The third section agrees with the book of Revelation in stating that there are 360 counted days in a year (1Eno 74:14/11 & 75:1 and Rev 11:2-3/12:6/13:5). Also, it is accurate in stating that in the time leading up to the great flood the perfect calendar Enoch was shown would be "altered" and the order of the sun will be changed –I.e. 364 days becoming 365.242199 days– because of sin (1Eno 80:4-7), but that we should still continue to use this 364 day calendar (1Eno 82:3-7) –verified in the fact that Yeshua used this calendar (in light of the information given in the "New Testament," secular historical sources, astronomical observations and the Dead Sea Scrolls). There is also ample evidence in Scripture that this calendar was used by ancient Israel (Gen 7:11;24/8:3-4 , 1Sa 20:5, 1Ch 27:1-15, 1Ki 4:7, Est 3:7, etc.).

In the fourth section of the book of 1Enoch, a parable is given that covers the time span from Noah until the end of the world and life in the new heaven and new earth. It foretells that there would be a remnant of faithful Israelites at the time of the Messiah's first coming (1Eno 90:6). It foretells the beheading of John the Baptist (1Eno 90:8). It predicts the first coming of Yeshua at that time (1Eno 90:9). It foretells Yeshua being a light to the lost sheep of the house of Israel (1Eno 90:9-10).

It predicts the death of Yeshua (1Eno 90:16). It predicts a destruction of Jerusalem and the **3rd** Temple (1Eno 90:28) –also predicted in Dan 9:26. It predicts a millennial reign (1Eno 90:29-30) –also foretold in Rev 20:4, 6, as well as an end time wedding feast (1Eno 90:32-34) –also predicted in Rev 19:6-9. It predicts that after this time, all eyes of Israel would be opened (1Eno 90:35-36) –predicted also in Isa 11:9, Jer 31:34 & Hab 2:14. Finally, it foretells an adoption taking place with Yeshua becoming the Lamb of Yah (Eno 90:37-39) –fulfilled in Yeshua (Joh 1:12, Rom 8:29, Rev 5:6).

The final section of the book is a timely warning to us who are living in the last days (Eno 91:7/108:1) to stay away from the ways of sinners because Yah will execute judgment on the sinners (1Eno 91:6-9, 92:5, 94:1, 95:5-7, 96:8, 97:3, 98:3, 99:1-16, 102:3, 103:8, 104:5, &108:3).

This section also foretells when events in history would transpire, with extreme Biblical accuracy.

(More information is provided later on in this chapter.)

It also speaks of the Torah being given for the sake of sinners (93:4) –information also given in 1Ti 1:9. It also speaks of the first resurrection of the dead and the eternal light we will be walking in (1Eno 91:10 & 92:3). It also speaks of the creation of the new heaven and new earth (1Eno 91:16). It also speaks of Yeshua as Yah's Son (1Eno 105:2).

R. H. Charles, a noted scholar, has documented 128 instances where the book of Enoch influences the "New Testament." Some of these instances may include: 1Eno 94:8 and Mat 6:19-24/19:23, 1Eno 94:11 and Mat 24:9/Jn 17:14, 1Eno 97:7 and Rev 10:1-5, 1Eno 108:3 and Rev 20:15, 1Eno 108:9 and Jn 12:25 and 1Eno 62:15 and Rev 7:13-14/20:4.

Perhaps the most influenced book of the "New Testament" on the book of Enoch is Revelation. For example, much of the concept of the lake of fire, described in the book of Revelation (Rev 19:20, 20:10, 15, 21:8), comes from the book of Enoch (Eno 10:13, 54, 67, 91:9, 98:3, 100:9, 108:2-7). Also, there are at least seven parallels in which the same words are used.

1) "And another messenger came and stood at the
    altar, holding a golden censer, and much incense
    was given to him, that **he should offer** it with the
    prayers of all the set-apart ones…and they cried
    with a loud voice, saying, "How long, O Master,
    set-apart and true, until You judge and avenge **our
    blood** on those who dwell on the earth?" …they
    were told that they should rest a little while longer,
    until both the number of their fellow servants and
    their brothers, who would be killed as they were,
    was **completed**."

    - Rev 8:3-4, 10-11

    "And in those days shall have ascended **the prayer
    of the righteous** and the blood of the righteous
    from the earth before Yah of Hosts. And the hearts
    of the holy were filled with joy; because the number
    of the righteous **had been offered**, and the prayer of
    the righteous had been heard, and the **blood of the
    righteous** been **required** before Yah of Hosts"

    -1Eno 47:1, 4

2) "And **out of His mouth goes a sharp sword**, that
    with it He should **smite the nations**. And He shall
    shepherd them with a rod of iron. And He treads
    the winepress of the fierceness and wrath of El
    Shaddai."

    -Rev 19:15

    "And Yah of Hosts seated [the Chosen One] on the
    throne of His glory, and the spirit of righteousness
    was poured out upon him, and the **word of his
    mouth slays all the sinners**."

    -1Eno 62:1-2

3) "And I saw the dead, small and great, standing before **the throne**, and **books were opened**"

-Rev 20:12

"… He seated himself upon **the throne** of His glory, and the **books of the living were opened**"

-1Eno 47:3

4) "And the sea **gave up the dead who were in it**, and death and **Sheol gave up the dead**"

-Rev 20:13

"And in those days shall the earth also **give back that which has been entrusted to it**, and Sheol **also shall give back**"

-1Eno 51:1

5) "And if anyone was **not found written in the Book of Life**, he was **thrown into the lake of fire**."

-Rev 20:15

…**their names shall be blotted out of the book of life** and…in the **fire shall they burn**"

-1Eno 108:3

6)   "And I saw a new heaven and **a new earth**...The one who overcomes shall inherit all this...**But** as for **the cowardly, and untrustworthy, and abominable, and murderers, and those who whore, and drug sorcerers, and idolaters, and all the false**, their part is in the lake which burns with fire and sulfur, which is the second death. And there **shall by no means enter**"

-Rev 21:1, 7-8, 27

"And I will **transform the earth** and make it a blessing: And I will cause Mine elect ones to dwell upon it: **But the sinners and evil-doers shall not set foot thereon.**"

-1 Eno 45:5

7)   "And he showed me a river of water of life, clear as crystal, coming from **the throne** of the Mighty One...In the middle of its street...was the **tree of life**...And the leaves of the tree were for the healing of the nations. And **no longer shall there be any curse**"

- Rev 22:1-3

"And as for this fragrant **tree**, no mortal is permitted to touch it till the great judgment... It shall then be given to the righteous and holy...it shall be **transplanted to the holy place**...and its fragrance shall be in their bones... and in **their days shall no** sorrow or **plague**"

- Eno 25:4-6

In addition to the Biblical credence to the book of Enoch, the book was regarded as Scripture by at least one group of devout Jews prior to the time of Yeshua (as evidenced in the Dead Sea Scrolls) and the Church up until the fifth century CE (as evidenced in the quotes of Athenagoras, Clement of Alexandria, Irenaeus, and Tertullian). The book of Enoch was removed from the canon by the prevailing Jewish body, namely the Pharisees, near the end of the first century CE. According to Tertullian, a second-to-third century church father, <u>the reason for this rejection of the book was that it clearly pointed to Yeshua as being the Messiah</u> (Ante-Nicene Fathers, Vol IV, Book I, Ch III).

With the exception of the Ethiopic Orthodox Church, the Church eventually followed suit in the fifth century, for some reason or another. As a result, the only complete text of the book of Enoch exists in the Ethiopic script.

The book of Enoch is arguably the most valuable book ever taken out of Scripture. It complements the canonized Scripture many ways. It gives explanatory details to topics such as: the tree of knowledge and the tree of life (Gen 2:9), the fallen angels (Gen 6:1-2, Dan 4:13, 17, 23), Azazel (Lev 16:8, 10, 26), Sheol (Luk 16:22-26), heaven (Eze 28:13-16), and Gehenna (Mat 18:9, etc.). It also lays out a perfect calendar, which would explain why Moses didn't have to. Finally, it also gives encouragement to obey Yah and believe in Yeshua to those who are living in the last days. From a purely Biblical perspective, there is no reason to reject any part of the book of Enoch as Scripture.

In Enoch 93:3-15(91:15), there is a vision given that deals with the history of man, which foretells when events in history would transpire, with extreme Biblical accuracy.

First, it must be observed that there are a total of ten weeks.

Next, it should be realized that each week is speaking of 700 years. So week 1 is years 0-699; week 2 is 700-1399; week 3 is 1400-2099; week 4 is 2100-2799; week 5 is 2800-3499; week 6 is 3500-4199; week 7 is 4200-4899; week 8 is 4900-5599; week 9 is 5600-6299; and week 10 is 6300-6999. All years given are AM (after creation).

Finally, verse 3 is speaking of Enoch, the seventh person from Adam (Jud 1:14). Once this is understood, we can see that:

It foretells that Abraham would be chosen around the year 2100 (93:5). According to Biblical chronology (MT, with no gaps of time), this happened around the year 2030.

It foretells that David would be given the promise of a Messianic heir near the year 2800 (93:6). According to Biblical chronology (MT, with no gaps of time), this happened around the year 2850.

It foretells that the second temple would be built around 3500 (93:7). According to Biblical chronology (MT, with no gaps of time), this happened around the year 3440.

It foretells that Yeshua would resurrect from the dead, that the second temple would be destroyed and that His original followers would be dispersed near the year 4000 (93:8), and that a corrupt church will arise shortly thereafter (1Eno 93:9). According to Biblical chronology (MT, with no gaps of time), all this happened around the years 3980 to 4050.

Finally, it foretells a period from around the years 6200-6900 (or 6000 to 7000), when Yeshua returns, righteousness prevails over wickedness and a final judgment takes place (91:14-15).

VII. Conclusion

Chapter 21

The Narrow Way

The key passage this chapter will look at is Mat 7:13-14:

> "Enter ye in at the strait gate...Because strait *is* the gate, and narrow *is* the way, which leads unto life, and **few there be that find it.**"

There are many religions out there. In addition to these recognized religions, there are other worldviews that are given titles such as 'theist,' 'atheist,' 'agnostic,' 'spiritual,' etc. Within many recognized religions, there are several sects or denominations.

Christianity, for example, has as many as 43,000 recognized and unrecognized denominations (as of 2012, according to The Center for the Study of Global Christianity at Gordon-Conwell Theological Seminary).

Just within Catholicism, the largest and most unified Christian denomination by far (representing over half of all Christians), there are 13 different recognized Catholic denominations. (This does not include those confined to a particular country, i.e. the Ethiopian Catholic Church.)

However, of all these religions, worldviews, and "religions within religions," according to Yeshua, there are only two ways:

The narrow way that leads to life
The broad way that leads to death

Yeshua said that there would be few who find the narrow way.

To get a perspective of what this proportion might look like, let us consider a passage of Scripture that Paul makes reference to in Romans 11:4.

The prophet Eliyah had just escaped from the wicked Jezebel. Yah had just appeared to him on three separate occasions. In his fourth and final visitation—speaking out of a still small voice, Yah utters these words (as recorded in 1Ki 19:18):

> *"Yet I have left me **seven thousand** in Israel, all the knees which have not bowed unto Baal, and every mouth which has not kissed him."*

At this point in Israel's history, we were "as **the sand of the sea**"(Isa 10:22)—an uncountable amount of people.

(There were less than 200 years from the time of Eliyah to the time of Isaiah.)

There is a prophecy in Deu 1:11 that Yah would multiply us by 1,000. In the wilderness when this prophecy was given we were as many as 10 million people—counting men, women, children and strangers (Num 26:51, 62 + 1 million women, 7 million children under the age of 20, and 1.37 million strangers). This estimate may be a little on the high end. To be extremely conservative, we will figure that there were only 3 million people (630,000 men, 630,000 women, 1 million children under 20 years of age, and 740,000 strangers).

At this time, this number was considered uncountable (Num 23:10, Deu 1:10). 1,000 times this number would be 3 billion people. Over a time span of about 3900 years—the time from Deu 1:11 to the return of Yeshua, this is an average growth rate of a little less than 26% per year.

If this growth rate had been consistent, we can calculate that at the time of 1Ki 19:18, there may have been about 400 million Israelites.

So the fraction would look like this:

7,000/400,000,000 = .00175%

If we were to extrapolate this to today, this is what Yah's faithful remnant would look like when looking at those who claim to follow the Messiah:

.00175% x 2,400,000,000 = **42,000**

This figure represents a proposal of Yah's faithful remnant alive today, **worldwide!**

While there are an estimated 7.4 billion people in the world, there are an estimated 2.4 billion Christians.

This means that about 1 out of every 3 people on the planet self-indentify as "followers of Christ."

"Many are called…" (Mat 20:16, 22:14, Luk 8:13-14)

However, about 1 out of every 1,750 people on the planet may end of being saved in the last day.

"…but few are chosen." (Mat 20:16, 22:14, Luk 8:15)

Suffice it to say; *few* means *few.*

This statistic represents a very unfortunate scenario. Hopefully, it is nowhere near the actual figure.

Even if half (that's being very generous) of all self-identified Christians are part of Yah's remnant, that would mean that less that 17% of the population of the planet are going to be saved in the last day.

This is not Yah's desire. He wishes that everyone would come to repentance and be saved and not perish (Eze 18:32, 1 Ti 2:4, 2 Pe 3:9).

He promises that those who diligently seek Him wholeheartedly will find Him and the narrow way.

> *"But if from thence you shall **seek Yah** your Mighty One**, you shall find him**, if you seek him **with all your heart** and with all your soul."*

> -Deu 4:29

> *"And ye shall **seek me, and find me**, when ye shall **search for me with all your heart**."*

> -Jer 29:13

*"For every one that asks receives; and he that **seeks** **finds**; and to him that knocks it shall be opened."*

-Mat 7:8

*"Because strait is the gate, and narrow is the way, which leads unto life, and few there be that **find** **it**."*

-Mat 7:14

This runs contrary to the idea of recruiting/converting anybody we can find. We <u>should</u> share our faith with everyone who is willing to listen. To those who are called to baptize, this can be in the form of street evangelism. But in the end, the responsibility of finding the Way rests not on us, but on them. After all, those of us who have found it did so because we were genuinely seeking truth.

What about self-labeling?

1Co 1:10-13

> "And I appeal to you, brothers, by the name of our Master Yeshua the Messiah, that you all agree, and that there are **no divisions among you**, <u>but that you be knit together in the same mind and in the same opinion.</u>
>
> For I have been informed concerning you, my brothers, by those of *the house of* Chloe, that there are strife among you. What I mean is this, that each one of you says, '**I am of Paul**,' or '**I am of Apollos**,' or '**I am of Peter**,' or
>
> '**I am of Messiah**.'
>
> Has the Messiah <u>been divided</u>? Was Paul crucified for you? Or were you immersed in the name of Paul?"

We should not call ourselves by any religious or denominational name; not even "of Christ" (Christian) or "of Messiah"(Messianic) (1Co 1:12). For in doing so, we are in danger of breaking the unity Yah has called us to—in Him (1:10, 3:6, Joh 17:11, & 21-23).

Peter seems to have borrowed the term "Christian" at one point (1 Pe 4:16) from the Assembly of Antioch (Act 11:26). However, he does not address "Christians" in either one of his letters. Instead, he writes to the "strangers" of this secular word (1 Pe 1:1, 2:11) and those "chosen" out of this world (1 Pe 1:2, 2:4, 9, 2 Pe 1:1, 3).

In addition to being "chosen" and "strangers," we can describe ourselves as:

- **His watchmen/branches** ("N'tzarim" in Hebrew)
  Isa 49:6, 60:21, Jer 31:6, Act 24:5, 14.

- **His children**
  Exo 4:22, Jer 31:9, Hos 1:10, 11:1, Joh 1:12-13,
  Rom 8:16-17, Co 6:18, Php 2:15, & 1Jn 3:12.

- **His remnant**
  Lev 26:44, Isa 1:9, 10:20-22, 11:11,16, 28:5, Jer
  23:3, 31:7, 42:2, Joe 2:32, Amo 9:12, Zep 3:13,
  Rom 9:27, 29, 11:5, Rev 12:17.

- **His students/disciples**
  Isa 8:16, 54:13, Mat 28:19, Act 1:15, 6:1, 7, 9:19,
  25, 26, 36, 11:29, 15:10, 16:1, 18:23, 27, 19:1, 9,
  20:7, 21:4, 16.

- **His people, faithful Israel**
  Exo 3:7, 10, 5:1, 7:16, 8:1, 20, 9:1, 10:3, Lev 26:12,
  Psa 50:7, 81:11, Isa 1:3, 10:24, 52:6, 65:19, Jer
  30:3, 31:1, 14, 33, 32:38, Hos 2:23, Zec 13:9, Rom
  9:25, 11:17, 2Co 6:16, Eph 2:11-13, Heb 8:10, Rev
  18:4.

- **His set-apart ones**
  Exo 19:6, Lev 11:44, 19:2, 20:7, Num 15:40, 16:3,
  30:4, 31:23, 34:9, 37:28, 52:9, Deu 7:6, 14:2, 21,
  26:19, 28:9, 33:3, Psa 16:3, 34:9, Isa 4:3, Dan 8:24,
  Hos 11:12, Mat 27:52, Act 9:13, 32, 41, 26:10,

Rom 1:7, 8:27, 12:13, 15:25, 26, 31, 16:15, Col 1:2,1 Co 6:1, 2, 14:33, 16:1, 2 Co 8:4, 9:1, 12, 13:13, Eph 1:1, 15, 18, 2:19, 3:8, 18, 4:12, 5:3, 6:18, Phi 1:1, 4:22, Col 1:2, 4, 12, 26, 1Th 3:13, 2Th 1:10, 1Ti 5:10, Phm 1:7, Heb 6:10, 23:24, Jud 1:3, Rev 5:8, 8:3, 4, 11:18, 13:7, 10, 14:12, 16:6, 17:6, 18:24, 19:8, 20:9.

- **Those who follow the Way of the Messiah**
  Exo 18:20, 32:8, Deu 4:9, 5:32, 8:6, 9:16, 10:12, 11:13, 16, 22, & 28, 13:3-5, 19:9, 26:17, 27:18, 28:9, & 14, 30:16, 31:29, Jos 1:7, 22:5, 23:6, Jdg 2:22, 1Sa 12:20, 1 Ki 2:3, 8:58, 2Ki 21:22, Psa 1:6, 25:9, 103:7, 119:1, 3, 14, 27, 30, 32, 33, 35, 125:5, 139:24, 143:8, Pro 2:20, 4:11, 25-27, 6:23, 8:20, 9:6, 10:17, 29, 12:28, 13:6, 15:10, 19, 24, 16:31, 21:16, 22:6, 23:19, Isa 2:3, 26:7, 28:7, 30:21, 40:3, 42:24, 43:19, 48:17, Jer 5:4, 5, 6:16, 21:8, 29:13, 42:3, Eze 18:25, 29, 33:17, 20, Mic 4:2, Hab 3:6, Mat 2:8, 3:1, 3, Mat 7:14, 21:32, 22:16, Mar 1:3, 12:14, Luk 1:76, 3:4, 20:21, 21:34, Joh 1:23, 14:6, Act 9:2, 18:25, 26, 19:9, 23, 22:4, 24:14, 22, Rom 3:12, 11:33, Heb 5:2, 12:13, 2Pe 2:2, & 21.

Chapter 22

The Broad Way

This chapter will be focusing on the bulk of 2 Thessalonians 2:1-12 and relating it to the "broad way" described in Mathew 7:13-23.

> "Now we beseech you, brethren, by **the coming of our Master Yeshua the Messiah**, and *by* our gathering together unto him, That ye be not soon shaken in mind, or be troubled, neither by spirit, nor by word, nor by letter as from us, as that the day of the Messiah is at hand. Let no man deceive you by any means: **for *that day shall not come,* except there come a falling away first,** and **that man of sin be revealed, the son of perdition;**

> Who opposes and exalts himself above all that is called Mighty, or that is worshipped; so that he as the Mighty One sits in the temple of the Mighty One, showing himself that he is the Mighty One. Remember ye not, that, when I was yet with you, I told you these things? And now ye know what withholds that he might be revealed in his time.

> For the mystery of lawlessness is already work: only he who now allows *will do so,* until he be taken out of the way.

And **then shall that lawless one be revealed**, whom **the Master shall consume with** the spirit of his mouth, and shall destroy with **the brightness of his coming**: *Even him,* whose coming is after the working of the satan with all power and signs and lying wonders, And with all deceivableness of unrighteousness in them that perish; because they received not the love of the truth, that they might be saved.

And for this cause the Mighty One shall send them <u>strong delusion</u>, that they should believe a lie: That they all might be damned who believed not the truth, but had pleasure in unrighteousness."

Several key points that can be gleaned from this passage:

1) Before the Messiah returns, the false Messiah will come (v3).

2) The false Messiah will be consumed by the Messiah when He returns (v8).

3) Leading up to the coming of the false Messiah will be a "falling away"/ "of lawlessness" (v3, 8).

4) This "falling away" had already begun when this letter was written (v7).

Seeing as how the *false* Messiah has not come; nor has **the** Messiah return, we can gather that the "falling away"/ "mystery of lawlessness" has persisted to this day, **since the time** the second letter to the Thessalonians was written.

Some "New Testament" scholars date 2 Thessalonians to as early as the year 50 CE, while others date it to as late as 115 CE.

What "falling away" has persisted to this day since the latter half of the first century or the beginning of the second century?

Second Bishop of Antioch, a man by the name of Ignatius (c35-c108) wrote seven letters the late first century and early second century church. In one such letter, the Epistle to the Magnesians, he writes:

> *"Be not deceived with strange doctrines, nor with old fables, which are unprofitable. For **if we still live according to the Jewish law**, we acknowledge that **we have not received grace.**"*
> (Chap 8)

> *"If, therefore, those who were brought up in the ancient order of things[7] have come to the possession of a new hope, **no longer observing the Sabbath**, but living in the observance of the **Lord's Day**, on which*

also our life has sprung up again by Him and by His death" (Chap 9)

*"Therefore, having become His disciples, let us learn to **live according to the principles of Christianity**. For whosoever is called by any other name besides this, is not of God. Lay aside, therefore, the evil, the old, the sour leaven, and be ye changed into the new leaven, which is Jesus Christ. Be ye salted in Him, lest anyone among you should be corrupted, since by your savor ye shall be convicted. It is absurd to profess Christ Jesus, and to Judaize. For **Christianity did not embrace Judaism, but Judaism Christianity**"* (Chap 10)

This is when and where (near end of first century, Antioch) Christianity started to become a **distinct** religion from the Way—Torah-keeping Jewish and Gentile believers of Yeshua (Rom 3:29, 9:24, 11:7&17-22, 1 Cor 10:32, 12:13, Eph 2:11-14).

At this time, the Assembly of Antioch ceased to observe the Sabbath, replacing it with Sunday, and rejected the rest of the law Yah gave to His people. In Ignatius's mind, this newly formed religion succeeded the Way.

Since this time, the religion of Christianity has had a long history consisting of many things. The overview includes: enduring persecution and martyrdom, "Christianizing" pagan customs, splitting, persecuting those of non-orthodoxy, engaging in "holy" wars, splitting again, executing "witches," persecuting and *burning* "heretics," Jews, homosexuals, and Native Americans *alive*, buying trading, and treating others of a different ethnicity as property, charity, prophesying, casting out demons, and performing miraculous works.

But through it all, the vast majority of Christianity has kept one thing—lawlessness (compare the Greek word used in 2Th 2:7 & Mat 7:23 with that of 1Jo 3:4).

They justify this lawlessness by citing Paul's writings that speak of the necessity of faith in the life of Yah's people.

Many even go so far as to turn the "grace" Paul spoke of (Rom 5:15 & Eph 2:8-9 for example) into **a license to sin** (compare Rom 3:8, 6:1, & 15 with Jud 1:4). While it would be difficult to find somebody who would *acknowledge* they are doing this, the same people have either directly cited Joh 1:17, Rom 6:14, Gal 2:21, 5:4, and/or Eph 2:8 to justify disobeying Yah's law (which according to Rom 3:20b, 7:7 & 1Jo 3:4, is sin), or would say that they are given "grace" when they are not in obedience to Yah's law.

This ultimately brings us to the prophecy given by Yeshua in Mat 7:13-23; that many will be led astray by false prophets who, in the end, will profess Him as their Master, but will be turned away because they do not do the Father's will by obeying His law.

"…broad *is* the way, that leads to destruction, and many there be which go in…beware of false prophets…Not every one that says unto me, Master, Master, shall enter into the kingdom of heaven; **but he that doeth the will of my Father**

…many will say to me in that day, Master, Master, have we not prophesied in your name? and in your name have cast out devils? and in your name done many wonderful works?

And then will I profess unto them, I never knew you: depart from me, **ye that work lawlessness**."

Why so much division?

Hopefully, all readers of this book can agree that it is Yeshua's desire that we all be united.

Joh 17:1, 11, 21, 22, 23

> *These words spoke Yeshua, and lifted up his eyes to heaven, and said:*
>
> *"...Holy Father, <u>keep</u> through your own name <u>those whom you have given me</u>, **that they may be one**, <u>as we are</u>*
>
> *...**That they all may be one**; <u>as you, Father, art in me, and I in you</u>, that **they also may be one** <u>in us</u>*
>
> *... **that they may be one**, <u>even as we are one</u>:*
>
> *I in them, and you in me, **that they may be made perfect in one.**"*

Hopefully, we can also agree that this is unfortunately not the case. As pointed out in chapter 21 (page 237) there is a very large amount of different sects in existence, all claiming to follow the same Book. Even if we were to only look at those who are part of the faithful remnant (or at least those who claim to be), there is much division. What gives?

How can there be so many people who interpret the objective Truth so subjectively?

Although a complex issue, I would like to propose that there are **two** root causes for this vast array of interpretations (that leads to division); that if corrected, can go a long way in bringing the unity that Yah desires of His people:

1) **Basing too many of our religious beliefs on what other people say or do.**

What makes this problem so vicious is that it builds on itself. For this reason, it is an easy trap to get caught into.

Over the last nearly 2,000 years, this pitfall has singlehandedly led to thousands of divisions.

Take, for example, just two people in the last 500 years of ecclesiastical history: Martin Luther and John Calvin.

These two men started a movement that popularized what the early church (pre-Augustine) labeled heresy: *that we cannot play any part in our salvation.* (See Ante-Nicene Fathers, Vol 3: Bk 2, Ch 5, v6-7, Ch 6, v6-8, Ch 7, v4, Ch 8, v1-3, Ch 9, v7-8, Ch 23, book IV, ch 7, 36, & 40, & Church Fathers: Against Heresies, Vol 3, Bk 4, Ch 29). As a result of just two men's teachings, hundreds of millions of Christians and "Messianics" have embraced this false teaching.

The first thing I said in this book is that I am just another person. My views may change over time as I continue to "strive to show myself approved" (2Ti 2:15).

I ask that you maintain the same attitude.

A late second-early third century believer named Tertullian, when speaking of the commonly known heretic Marcion, wrote the following (Tertullian: Against Marcion, Bk 4, Ch 4):

> *"I say that my Gospel is the* true *one; Marcion, that his is. I affirm that* Marcion's Gospel *is adulterated; Marcion, that mine is. Now what is to settle the point for us, except it be that principle of time, which rules that the authority lies with that which shall be found to be more ancient; and assumes as an elemental* truth, *that corruption (of doctrine) belongs to the side which shall be convicted of comparative lateness in its origin. For, inasmuch as* error *is falsification of* truth, *it must needs be that* truth, *therefore, precedes* error. "

This is a good argument. It makes sense.

How do we determine whose Biblical interpretation is correct over another, opposing interpretation; but by looking at which interpretation came first?

To this end, I recommend reading a book entitled *Will the Real Heretics Please Stand Up*. In 158 short pages, the author shares his research into the second-century church's beliefs and practices to compare them to those of the church of today. Although the second-century church (post-Ignatius) had already begun drifting away from Yah's law, they certainly have the advantage of time over us. They were, in some cases, the immediate disciples of Yeshua's immediate disciples. Polycarp is a good example. Clement of Rome may be another good example.

However, these men (Polycarp, Clement of Rome, Theophilus, Hegesippus), nor the well known "Torah teachers" of today, should be elevated to the place of Yeshua (1 Co 1:10-13 & 1 Co 3:4-6)

Beyond the qualified elders of **our own** congregations, we should not so much as listen to these "teaching ministers"! (Please refer to chapter 9.) Unity in the Body of the Messiah begins with the local congregation.

Another way this primary cause leads to division is when we base our beliefs and actions on what other people *do*.

A couple of common examples of this are:

"David killed people, so there is nothing wrong with me killing people." (In the context of what laws of the land consider self-defense— which includes if someone has broken into your house, but you or your family's lives are not threatened and you know it).

"Abraham was a rich man, so there is nothing wrong with me desiring to be rich."

"Esther adorned herself with earrings and makeup, so there is nothing wrong with me getting dolled up."

"The Proverbs 31 woman was a bread-winner in her house, so there is nothing wrong with me, a woman, desiring a career outside the home."

All people, including Abraham, Esther, David, and the imaginary "Proverbs 31 woman" are sinful human beings. Not one of us is perfect.

For this reason, we should not try to justify our beliefs on the actions of others. The only Person in all history who is worth imitating is Yeshua.

This is particularly the case if the thing we are using to justify our beliefs or actions is contrary to Biblical teaching. For the first example, Scripture clearly teaches us not to desire to be rich (Mat 6:19-24, 1 Ti 6:5-10, 1 Co 6:10, Eph 5:5, Col 3:5). For the second example, Scripture clearly teaches us not to be violent with our enemies (Mat 5:39, 44, Rom 12:9) and not to take human life (Gen 9:6, Deu 32:39, Mat 26:52). For the third example, Scripture clearly teaches women to dress modestly (1 Pet 3:3-4, 1 Ti 2:9-10). For the last example, Scripture clearly teaches women to have children (1 Ti 5:14, 1 Ti 2:15, Tit 2:4) and keep their homes (Tit 2:5).

Although difficult to accept by many, this must be understood and practiced if we want to be Yeshua's disciples (Joh 8:31) and be unified in Him.

2) Basing too many of our religious beliefs on personal feelings.

This problem is also tough to correct. We are all emotional beings to some extent. That is how we are wired. However, with Yah's help and with much discipline, we can each train ourselves not to allow our experiences and sentiments to interfere with our acceptance of the teachings of Scripture. We must understand that all Scripture is given to us for "teaching, reproof, correction, and instruction" in His ways (2 Ti 3:16).

We must realize that: as important as it is for us to sustain ourselves with food, we must apply <u>all</u> Scripture to our lives (Deu 8:3, Mat/Luk 4:4). We must submit <u>every part</u> of our lives, including our feelings, to Him and His communication to us—the 66 books of the Bible.

When we, as the scattered and divided Body, repent from our sin and <u>collectively</u> return to Yah, He will send Yeshua to earth again to bring us back to the Promised Land.

This will happen in the last days. Those who repent and unite as one people will be a **small**, faithful remnant.

Deu 4:27-31

> And Yah shall scatter you among the nations, and you shall be left <u>few in number</u> among the nations, where Yah shall lead you. And there you shall serve Mighty Ones, the work of men's hands, wood, and stone, which neither see, nor hear, nor eat, nor smell. But if from there you shall seek Yah your Mighty One, you shall find *him,* if you seek him with all your heart and with all your soul.
>
> When you art in tribulation, and all these things are come upon you, *even* <u>in the latter days</u>, if you **turn to Yah your Mighty One**, and shall be obedient unto his voice; (for Yah your Mighty One *is* a merciful Mighty One) he will

not forsake you, neither destroy you, nor forget the covenant of your fathers which he swore unto them. And shall **return unto Yah your Mighty One**, and shall obey his voice according to all that I command you this day, you and your children, with all your heart, and with all your soul; That <u>then Yah your Mighty One will turn your captivity</u>, and have compassion on you, and will return <u>and gather you from all the nations</u>, from where Yah your Mighty One has scattered you.

Hos 3:5

"Afterward **shall the children of Israel return**, and seek Yah their Mighty One, and [the Messiah] their king; and shall fear Yah and his goodness <u>in the latter days</u>."

Hos 5:15

"I will go *and* return to my place, <u>till they acknowledge their offense</u>, and seek my face: in their affliction, **they will seek me early**."

Isa 11:11, 16

"And it shall come to pass in that day; that **Yah shall set his [Messiah] again the second time to recover the remnant** of his people, which shall be left…from the islands of the sea

And **there shall be a highway for the remnant** of his people…like as it was…in the day that [Israel] came up out of the land of Egypt."

I would like to leave you with a final challenge. The ancient Israelites were given the same challenge through the prophet Jeremiah.

My question to you is this: will *your* response to this challenge be the same as theirs?

Jer 6:16

> Thus says Yah, "Stand you in the ways, and see, and <u>ask for the old paths</u>, where *is* **the** good **Way**, and <u>walk therein</u>, and ye shall find rest for your souls."

> But they said "We will not walk *therein.*"

Intentionally, this book has no copyright. If you have been blessed through anything in this book, please share it with someone you care about. For a free pdf, or a hard copy at printing costs, feel free to email me at:

wayofthemessiah@outlook.com

Furthermore, if you desire to be part of a congregation that resembles those formed by the apostles of Yeshua, please contact me at the same email address.

Finally, feedback is always welcomed. If you wish to do so, please direct all feedback to this email address.

Yah bless!

-A Voice in the Wilderness